Cultivating Suicide?

Pressure Points in Irish Society

General Series Editor:
Professor Malcolm MacLachlan
Department of Psychology,
Trinity College Dublin

Titles in the Series:

Cultivating Suicide? Destruction of Self in a Changing Ireland
by Caroline Smyth, Malcolm MacLachlan and Anthony Clare
(ISBN 1-904148-15-8)

The Politics of Drugs: From Production to Consumption
by Peadar King (ISBN 1-904148-19-0)

Forthcoming Titles:

Refuge in Ireland: Myth and Reality
by Treasa Galvin

The Changing Face of Irish Authoritarianism
by Michael O'Connell

Pressure Points in Irish Society

Cultivating Suicide?

Destruction of Self in a Changing Ireland

Caroline Smyth
Malcolm MacLachlan
Anthony Clare

The Liffey Press

Published by
The Liffey Press Ltd
Ashbrook House, 10 Main Street
Raheny, Dublin 5, Ireland
www.theliffeypress.com

A catalogue record of this book is
available from the British Library.

ISBN 1-904148-15-8

Printed in the Republic of Ireland by Colour Books Ltd.

Contents

About the Authors .... *vii*

Acknowledgements .... *viii*

Series Introduction .... *ix*

Chapter 1: What is Suicide? **1**
- A Brief History of Suicide 6
- Defining Suicide 10

Chapter 2: Irish Suicide **15**
- Language, Mythology and Folklore 15
- The Unconfessed Sin and Fasting upon the Enemy 19
- Suicide in Contemporary Ireland 22

Chapter 3: Why Culture? **29**
- African American Culture 32
- Native American Culture 33
- Aotearoa's Maori Culture 39
- The Functions of Culture 40
- When Cultures Change 45
- "Celtic Tiger" Acculturation 48
- Anomie 51

Chapter 4: Why Youth? **57**
- A Newly Created Life-stage 57
- Adolescence as Pathology? 60
- Childhood Suicide 61
- Adolescent Suicide 67
- Youth Culture 72

Rock 'n' Roll and Youth Suicide:
Specific Elements of Youth Culture ... 73
Copycat Suicide and Media Coverage ... 75
Cultural Continuity as Suicide Prevention ... 78

Chapter 5: Why Gender? ... 83
The Gendering of Suicide ... 84
Whither "Man"? ... 87
Male Risk ... 92
Reconsidering Masculinity? ... 99

Chapter 6: Why Suicide? ... 107
Towards Prevention ... 107
A Schematic of Suicide ... 108
Shifting the Focus ... 115
Identifying Youth at Risk ... 117
Conclusion ... 123

References ... 127

Index ... 143

About the Authors

Caroline Smyth is a graduate student in the Department of Psychology, Trinity College Dublin. She is currently carrying out research in the area of adolescent suicide and culture change for her PhD. Other research interests include the impact of culture change on mental health and adolescent mental health. She is a member of the International Association of Cross-Cultural Psychology, the Irish Association of Suicidology and the Psychological Society of Ireland.

Malcolm MacLachlan is Associate Professor of Psychology and a Fellow of Trinity College Dublin and the Psychological Society of Ireland. He has published extensively on the interplay between culture and health, international aid and development, and embodiment in physical rehabilitation. Recent books include *Cultivating Pluralism: Psychological, Social and Cultural Perspectives on a Changing Ireland* (with Michael O'Connell, Oak Tree Press, 2000), *Cultivating Health: Cultural Perspectives on Promoting Health* (Wiley, 2001) and *Enabling Technologies: Body Image and Body Function* (with Pamela Gallagher; Churchill Livingstone, 2003). He is Visiting Clinical Psychologist at Cappagh National Orthopedic Hospital and is currently Chairperson of the National Committee for the Economic and Social Sciences.

Anthony Clare is a Consultant Psychiatrist at St Patrick's Hospital, Adjunct Professor of Psychiatry in Trinity College Dublin and Fellow of the Royal College of Psychiatrists, Royal College of Physicians Ireland and Royal College of Physicians (UK). He has published extensively on depression, alcohol abuse, chronic fatigue and allied subjects and has written a number of books on mental health, public understandings of psychiatry and men in contemporary society.

Acknowledgements

We would like to thank the following people who gave so generously of their time and advice in the course of writing this book: Derek Chambers (National Suicide Review Group); Tony Coughlan and Jim Dillon (Central Statistics Office); Enda McDonagh and Amanda Kracen.

We owe a huge debt of gratitude to Deirdre Desmond, Olga Horgan, Karen Smyth, Anne Walsh-Daneshmandi and Fergal Rooney. As colleagues and, more importantly, friends, your support, understanding and advice is invaluable and never ceases to amaze — so, "Thank You!" Sincere thanks also to Kieran Mulvey for his encouragement and constant supply of unique perspectives.

Thanks also to David Givens and Brian Langan at The Liffey Press for their professionalism, efficiency and warmth.

Finally, we gratefully acknowledge that the writing of this book has been partially supported by funding awarded to Caroline Smyth by the National Children's Office, and by a Berkeley Fellowship awarded to Malcolm MacLachlan by Trinity College Dublin.

Caroline Smyth
Malcolm MacLachlan
Anthony Clare
Dublin, 2003

SERIES INTRODUCTION

The *Pressure Points in Irish Society* series presents concise critical commentaries on social issues of contemporary concern. These books are written to be accessible, topical and, if necessary, controversial. Their aim is to "add value" to social debate by highlighting neglected issues, developing new perspectives on an existing debate or presenting new data that can enlighten our thinking. Each of the topics addressed in the series in some sense challenges complacency, upsets a sense of social equilibrium or questions the status quo. In short, *Pressure Points* is concerned with those issues that suggest "everything is not OK".

The term "pressure point" can of course mean different things in different contexts. One meaning of a "pressure point" is an issue that can be targeted by political pressure or influence. However, for many important social issues, political pressure is often not mounted by those within the political establishment, but rather by specific pressure groups, non-governmental organisations, community actions or campaigning individuals. The reluctance of many politicians to "make an issue" out of problems such as drugs, suicide, disability or immigration — to name but a few — is probably because they see them as quagmires from which there is no easy exit; or perhaps more cogently, no easy "exit poll" for their political savvy to weigh up. Many of our most destructive social issues are quite simply not vote winners. In the sense of applying pressure in the body politic, then, *Pressure Points* hopes to highlight issues that have been insufficiently debated, or considered in a blinkered fashion.

Another meaning of "pressure point", in the "body physical", as it were, is a place on the body where an artery can be pressed against a bone in order to stop bleeding. This calls forth the spectre of a system haemorrhaging and needing acute intervention. Here, there is not only a sense of immediacy, but also of weakness in one system threatening the viability of the whole body. Systems theory, of course, conceptualises problems not as singular entities but as interconnected and mutually reinforcing or diminishing phenomenon. Such thinking is central to the practice of social sciences: problems need to be considered in a broad societal context, rather than being seen as discrete entities in isolated systems working away on their own.

While the Chinese wish "may you live in interesting times", we in Ireland certainly do. The advent of the so-called "Celtic Tiger" brought us economic prosperity undreamt of a mere decade earlier. The uneasy "Peace Process" has arrested the relentless and senseless demeaning of an island soaked in the blood of its intolerance. The hitherto unanticipated net migration into Ireland has transformed our image of an island to "leave from", to one of an island to "arrive at". This has presented us with new challenges and opportunities, not least the opportunity to see our own cultural conflict in a much broader perspective. As such, the call for pluralism in Ireland not only offers a warmer and more considered welcome to immigrants, but also a warmer and more considered welcome to the "others" within our island.

Alongside economic prosperity and the peace process, we have also experienced a decline in the iconography of traditionally significant social figures. Priests, doctors, politicians and other stalwarts of the social order have, at least as collective entities, fallen from a presumption of benevolence, propriety and public service. Some of our priests have abused the trust of a nation and raped the innocence of our children; many doctors (and others) extort fees for private consultations and in so doing further undermine the public services they are handsomely paid to provide; while some politicians have been found to be up to their necks in corruption. Such events have profoundly affected the presumption of living in a pro-social "civil" society. Collective identity and the fear of God have giving way to individuation and the fear of negative equity, in lives now mortgaged to the hilt. Economic success has congested our cities, recast our social values and provided a materialistic common denominator into which our "value" is being weighed up.

It is the nature of any rapidly changing society that while some social virtues are lost, others are gained. People now feel they have greater civil liberties, greater access to the previously secret workings of the state, freedom to divorce, freedom to cohabit and have children out of wedlock and recently (and perhaps most dramatically), freedom to demonstrate their overwhelming wish that our government not facilitate war. Ultimately, it is not change *per se* that is good or bad, right or wrong, moral or immoral, but how we adapt to our new circumstances. It has always been the "job" of culture to make the lives of its members meaningful and to offer them guidelines for living — feeling valued and having a place in the world. The reach of globalisation, with its myriad mechanisms, such as the internet, television, and retail outlets, presents us afresh with the perennial challenge of deciding what we are about. Yet this need for identity, for rootedness, occurs in a completely new global context, with new "free trade" masters in a world pulsating to corporate interests, in an enlarged European Union in which we will inevitably have less influence.

How we respond to the pressure points in Irish society will define who we are and what factors are most influential over us. While a concern over how a small island like Ireland responds to global challenges may seem to be rather a parochial concern, in fact it is not. The world is made up of small communities with ethnic, religious and sometimes national identities. How local systems interact with global systems is of worldwide interest, as is captured by that ugly term "globalisation". Our concerns in Ireland may well be particular, but how we adapt to global issues is of general interest and importance. Many of the titles in this series arise from the local presentation of issues of global import.

I am very pleased to be associated with The Liffey Press's series on *Pressure Points in Irish Society*. We hope that in a modest way these books will advance thinking and practice in their target areas and that you will enjoy reading them and be enlivened by them. Finally, I invite all interested parties, from all walks of life, who have the drive to tackle such issues in a critical and concise manner, to join us by submitting a proposal to myself or to The Liffey Press, for a future book in this series.

Malcolm MacLachlan,
Department of Psychology,
Trinity College Dublin.

To my Mom,
who is without doubt the most interesting person I know,
for all your love.

Caroline Smyth

Chapter 1

What is Suicide?

Why did you give no hint that night
That quickly after the morrow's dawn,
And calmly, as if indifferent quite,
You would close your term here, up and be gone
Where I could not follow
With wing of swallow
To gain one glimpse of you ever anon!

Never to bid good-bye,
Or lip me the softest call,
Or utter a wish for a word, while I
Saw morning harden upon the wall,
Unmoved, unknowing
That your great going
Had place that moment, and altered all.

— Thomas Hardy, from "The Going"

Some years ago John[1] *was referred to one of us*[2] *after he made a failed suicide attempt. In response to the question "Could you tell me when you started to feel so down?" he responded, "It all began when I started to wear a tie"! I could not help smiling and, mercifully, the sense of humour that had made him so popular with his friends, still flickered, and he returned my smile. John's analysis of his distress was spot on. He was an intelligent, jovial and outgoing young man who did not like school, and took a job in a local supermarket when he was sixteen. There he made good friends,*

[1] Names and some details have been changed to protect anonymity.

[2] Malcolm MacLachlan.

enjoying a busy social life with workmates and going out with Mary, who was a year older than him and worked as a cashier.

When John reached nineteen he was promoted and given charge of eight staff, one of whom was a replacement for himself. In line with his increased responsibility, and greater status, he was asked to wear a tie. Slowly he became somewhat distant from the people he was in charge of and found it difficult to allocate people shifts that they didn't want. He resented friends thinking that he could rearrange work schedules just to accommodate their needs. Things became more difficult when one of his staff was sacked for stealing goods. Gradually over time, his former friends stopped inviting him to socialise with them after work, his girlfriend felt increasingly awkward about "sleeping with your boss" jokes and said that his promotion had changed him and that he "wasn't any fun anymore". Mary broke off their relationship.

John began to focus increasingly on just doing his job and it was hinted to him that he might be in line for another promotion soon. His parents, with whom he lived, were delighted with his success in work, and he felt unable to talk to them about his anguish and how he wished that he still had his old job. Over a period of a couple of months John became increasingly socially isolated, and when he did go out in the evening, would find a perch in the bar and drink to excess, which further distanced him from the friends he formerly socialised with.

After a night of heavy drinking and feeling dismal and desperate, John headed home across the bridge that spanned a broad river which ran through the town. Although he had thought about killing himself before, he was never that serious about it and could think of reasons not to do so. Now he could think of no reasons not to. Full of drink, he climbed over the side of the bridge, ensured that he was right in the middle of the river and let go of life, dropping twenty feet into the water.

The reason John was able to tell this story was that he, like some others before him, had not realised just how shallow the river was. As he waded through the thick mud and two and a half feet of water, John felt no relief, just stupidity: "I couldn't even do that right."

John was lucky, very lucky. He sprained an ankle and cracked a rib and it was that which routed him to me through his GP. Four days later, he was sitting there telling me this story. So, he was right: in a way it did all start with him wearing a tie.

This book is about how cultural change in Ireland may disorient people, how it may slowly unhinge them from traditional social values and supports that perhaps have never been known to have any explicit link to mental health or suicide. The reason we wanted to begin with a case study was to acknowledge that while a socio-cultural analysis of suicide may seem somewhat distant and "academic", our concern must be to apply this level of analysis to the personal tragedy of those drawn towards suicide and that ultimately, influencing how individuals react to changes in their *social* lives will be central to the prevention of suicide. Perhaps just as John's tie was symbolic of the new role and social isolation he came to experience as a result of his promotion, so too John's story may be symbolic of how, as a society, rushing into a "better future", we may have severed the very links that bound us together, and in so doing have denied some people the sort of life they would wish for.

Charles Handy, in his book *The Empty Raincoat* (1994), uses the metaphor of an upstanding raincoat that is occupied by no one to convey the sense of people fulfilling work roles that fail to contribute to their personal sense of meaning. He writes:

> To me, that empty raincoat is the symbol of our most pressing paradox. We were not destined to be empty raincoats, nameless numbers on a payroll, role occupants, the raw material of economics or sociology, statistics in some government report. If that is to be the price, then economic progress is an empty promise. There must be more to life than to be a cog in someone else's great machine. . . . (1994, pp. 1–2)

To be more precise, we would say, "there must be more to life than being a cog in a machine working against you, or feeling that you are not needed by the machine". We will argue that the "machine of life" is oiled by cultural identity and when that is undermined so is one's sense of value, belonging, meaning. Yet we do not propose some sort of cultural atavistic regression as a remedy. Rather, the challenge we lay down to Irish society is to move forward in a way that cultivates meaning and value for all. As such, we are interested in designing cultures for the future, in particular ones that minimise the propensity for suicide.

Some suicides, of course, have nothing to do with social change, culture or estrangement from family, friends or lovers. Indeed the weakness of a psychosocial analysis of the role of Irish cultural change in suicide is that it will necessarily make broad brushstrokes. That is, it is unlikely to "explain" particular acts of suicide, or the often heartbreaking circumstances in which they occur. Indeed such explanations are elusive and may often go to the grave, perhaps without even being understood by the victims themselves, or indeed the "other victims" — those they leave behind. In this book we do not set out to account for individual suicidal acts, or acts of attempted suicide; instead we want to understand why suicide has increased so dramatically over the last ten years in particular.

Suicide is not just a medical or psychological problem of the individual. It is more than that — it is a problem of society. However, it is not only the massive increase in suicide over recent years that we believe points to the importance of understanding the influence of cultural factors, it is also the demographics of who commits suicide: why, for instance, should Ireland have one of the highest male to female ratio for suicide in Northern Europe? Why do relatively more young Irish men kill themselves than any other nationality in Europe?

If, as we argue here, suicide can be "created" or "encouraged" by certain social conditions, then is it also something that can be challenged and reduced by the recognition of these conditions *and* a deliberate and focused effort to change them? That Irish society has changed, and will continue to do so, is clear. There is nothing wrong with culture change *per se*, especially when it helps people adapt to broader changes in their world. Whether we are prepared to let our citizenry become victims of such change, or whether we are prepared to "get in the driving seat" and direct such change, is the key issue. In this book we sketch out an argument that cultural factors have always had an important influence on suicide in Ireland, and that they will continue to do so.

Perhaps surprisingly, the approach we take here (where *both* the individual and the world that surrounds them are considered) is not one that has been widely adopted in recent times, either in Ireland or internationally. While this is now changing, it reflects a certain reluctance in the examination of social and cultural issues. In short, there has been a tendency to reduce suicide to the "mad", "bad", "sad" or "criminal", sooner than examine what, within our society, might be responsible for this growing social issue.

Internationally, a cultural perspective needs to be given more credence. Although we supplement our analysis of suicide and Irish cultural change by considering comparative experiences in other parts of the world, this book is primarily, and unashamedly, about Ireland. We believe that in Ireland and beyond, a great deal can be learnt from a "case study" of Ireland, of how the country has come to occupy such an undesirable place in the morbid statistics of suicide.

Our aim then is to convince the reader that radical and challenging initiatives that explicate the role of Irish culture in suicide must be taken. In the final chapter, we argue that this must be done in many ways and in many places, but especially in schools. We will not escape suicide by hiding from it or fearing to name it. We need to give people the tools to combat it. This is *not* a self-help book for the individual who is contemplating suicide, rather we would see it as more of a *help-yourself* book for a *society which is failing to contemplate it*. In the final chapter we therefore outline what we think would be necessary initiatives to address suicide at a societal level, and how and at whom such initiatives should be targets.

In the remainder of this chapter, we give a very brief history of suicide from ancient to modern times, and indicate how it has socially evolved from an act that was not condemned to one which was vilified. As the "meaning" of suicide has thus evolved, we also give our definition of suicide and distinguish it from other terminology, such as "self-harm". In the second chapter, we focus exclusively on the Irish situation and the way in which the meaning of suicide has changed over the past few centuries. Having set suicide in a historical and contextual perspective, we ask three simple questions: Why culture? Why youth? Why gender? Chapter 3 critically examines the value of a cultural investigation of suicide, with Chapter 4 focusing specifically on issues of youth suicide. Chapter 5 explores possible reasons for the very high rate of male suicide in particular. Chapter 6 condenses our previous review and argument in asking "Why Suicide?" It also outlines our urgent need to actively address suicide in Ireland through education and prevention, how we are failing to do this and how it might be done.

A Brief History of Suicide

The ancient Greeks reported suicide in a rather objective way, recording no moral judgement or condemnation of the act, but this is not to say that all suicides were met with equanimity (O'Connor and Sheehy, 2000). Acceptable and unacceptable motives for suicide were recognised. Suicide was "appropriate" in response to grief or threat of dishonour but was thought to be "inappropriate" in response to "lesser" experiences such as cowardice. But, for the most part, suicide was an everyday part of life and was not seen as a reflection of abnormality or pathology. In a similar vein, the Romans looked upon suicide as a further reflection of the way in which they lived. A suicide, when motivated by those values held in high esteem, was seen as an honourable death. Interestingly, the suicide of a slave was seen as irrational and selfish (to use modern terms) as this deprived society of a useful worker and thus, valuable property. The life of a slave was not their own, and therefore not their own to take! Suicide by soldiers (whose lives served the purpose of the state) were viewed in a similar manner (Spellissy, 1996).

The word "suicide" first appeared in *Religio Medici* by Sir Thomas Browne (1605–1682) (Shneidman, 1985). While one could carry out acts of "self-slaughter", "self-killing" and "self-destruction" (Alvarez, 1971) thus implying the act, suicide was simply not possible. Authors such as Shneidman argue that a secular view of the world was required before suicide could come to be. For as long as a medieval view of humanity's existence, the role of God and the reality of an afterlife was unquestioningly held, one could end one's life on earth but could not forever cease to be. Only when a questioning of these beliefs took place could suicide be named. If there were no God, no heaven and no eternal existence, then the individual (playing an active role in the determination of their own fate) could choose to die, forever terminating their existence and, in modern terms, commit suicide.

Many philosophers have written about suicide. Shneidman (1985) draws attention to Pythagoras, Plato, Aristotle, Socrates, Seneca, Epictetus, Descartes, Spinoza, Voltaire, Hume, Kant, Kierkegaard and Rousseau, each of whom have had something to say on the issue. For our purposes, to develop a socio-cultural perspective, it is perhaps the opinion of the last-named Rousseau (1712–1778) which is most relevant, as he transferred sin from man to society, thus beginning a more sociological view of the phenomenon. This is an approach also favoured by Hume (1783/1929) in the piece "An Essay On Suicide", published a year after his death, which proposes that suicide is neither a crime nor a dereliction of duty at any level. From this perspective, to take one's own life was not to express a selfish disregard for oneself, one's society or even God. Rather, it was a logical and reasonable action to rid oneself of life, if existence has become an unbearable burden.

In the Western world, the attitude of the Christian church has had an enormous influence on how we think about suicide. The Old Testament contains several references to suicide, perhaps one of the most explicit being 2 Samuel 17:23:

> When Achit'ophel saw that his counsel was not followed, he saddled his ass, and went off home to his own city. And he set his house in order, and hanged himself.

Examples from the New Testament, although not as frequent (the only mentioned case is that of Judas Iscariot), serve a clear purpose, placing suicide firmly alongside the notions of betrayal and shame. Thus the position of the traditional Roman Catholic Church is undeniably clear. St Augustine (354–430 AD) was concerned with suicides only of a certain type (those associated with martyrdom). The result is that suicides for reasons of intolerable circumstances, emotional suffering, old age, personal honour or illness were not the subject of St Augustine's writings (Shneidman, 1985). Nonetheless, he went so far as to assert that the suicide of Judas Iscariot was a crime more heinous even than the betrayal of Christ (Kelleher, Keeley, Chambers, and Corcoran, 2000), making the view of this time undoubtedly clear. Further to this, a series of Church councils established a formal church position on suicide. The Council of Arles (452 AD) saw suicide censured as the murder of an innocent (Silviny, 1957), while the Council of Orleans (533 AD) prohibited suicide victims from being buried on consecrated ground (O'Connor and Sheehy, 2000). This was followed by the Council of Braga (562 AD) which called for a general denial of burial rites (including rites of Eucharist and the singing of Psalms) for those who committed suicide (Grullman, 1971) and subsequently, the Council of Toledo (693 AD), required those who even attempted suicide to be excommunicated from the Church.

By the time Thomas Aquinas (1929) came to make proclamations on the act, the sixth commandment had undergone a reinterpretation with "thou shalt not kill" having been extended to include oneself as much as others. His argument consisted of three principle elements. The first was that death was contrary to everything in nature, which will strive to survive for as long as possible, thus suicide goes against nature. Secondly, that we all exist as part of a greater whole (i.e. society) and so, to take one's own life is to deprive others (hence, a selfish act with no regard for others). The third aspect of Aquinas' argument was that, since all life is given by God, it is up to God (and Him alone) to take it — thus making suicide a sin against God. By this time, Aquinas was preaching to an already-converted choir as the relationship between sin and suicide had by then been firmly "established".

While such information might appear to be somewhat irrelevant to a modern consideration of suicide, it is important to remember the continued role of the Church (especially in a traditionally devout nation such as Ireland) and the impact the religious approach to suicide will have on those left behind. Rather than these "Christian" pronouncements originating from a respect for life and a reverence for the God-given state, Shneidman (1985) and others have argued that they were instead clearly motivated by more political and practical factors.

While Stillion and McDowell (1996) have argued that the twentieth-century Church relaxed the punitive attitudes of previous generations, insofar as there has been a move towards seeing the suicidal individual as being of unsound mind and thus, not capable of conscious sin, Bowers (1994) cites the Roman Catholic Universal Catechism of 1994, which continues to state that "suicide contradicts the natural human inclination to preserve and perpetuate life" and is "contrary to the love of a willing God" (p. 13). In a more positive vein, Spellissy (1996) reports that the Universal Catechism offers some hope stating:

> we should not despair of the eternal salvation of persons who have taken their own lives. By ways known to him alone can God provide the opportunity for salutary repentance. The church prays for persons who have taken their own lives.

While it would seem that the twenty-first century Church has come to present an appearance of greater acceptance and tolerance, it has not left the past completely behind and, while the issue of unsound mind may perhaps preclude the possibility of sin, it continues to portray suicide as an act of irrationality and "madness".

Curran (1987, p. 3) presents a case that further illustrates the dichotomy in thinking that has long surrounded suicide. A rather gruesome incident in 1860 England was reported by Nicholas Ogarev, a Russian travelling abroad, in a letter home:

> Apparently, a man was to be hanged for the crime of having attempted suicide, by cutting his own throat. Though the court was warned by its physician that hanging would prove fruitless since the man's mended throat would tear open from the hanging, allowing him to breathe through the aperture and survive, he was, nonetheless, hanged anyway. He survived. Amidst much consternation and dismay, the officials deliberated upon what to do next. Ultimately, the man's neck was bound up below the wound and held tight until he died, executed for suicide. The Russian observer comments in his letter, "Oh my Mary, what a crazy and stupid civilisation".

In this brief introductory chapter we have illustrated how the act of taking one's own life has evolved from, at times, being viewed as an honourable decision among the ancients, to being evidence of a criminal and evil propensity, punishable by death. It is through recognising such contrasts that we can understand how particular acts can be socially constructed to "mean" different things. As we shall see in Chapter 3, this is not simply a product of the passage of time — the difference between "then" and "now" — but that the meaning of suicide is also dependent upon cultural context — the difference between here and there. To conclude this introductory chapter, we set out just what exactly we mean by "suicide".

DEFINING SUICIDE

> Surely "suicide" is one of those patently self-evident terms, the definition of which, it is felt, need not detain a thoughtful mind for even a moment (Shneidman, 1985, p. 6).

It is widely accepted that the role of *intent* is fundamental in determining a suicidal act. In this light, it is argued that suicide is "a self-chosen behaviour that is intended to bring about one's own death in the short(est) term" (Diekstra, 1994). The issue of intent is placed to the fore with this definition and relied upon to make a determination of suicide. This is a view echoed by the World Health Organisation's definition (presented as part of the "World Health Report" (2001) which states that suicide is "the result of an act deliberately initiated and performed by a person in the full knowledge or expectation of outcome".

However, Shneidman (1985, p. 203) provides a more unifying, inclusive, flexible and purposive definition:

> currently in the Western World, suicide is a conscious act of self-induced annihilation, best understood as a multidimensional malaise in a needful individual who defines an issue for which the suicide [*sic*] is perceived as the best solution.

Several aspects of the definition are important to recognise. The first is that suicide is placed in a temporal and cultural context (*currently . . . Western world)* leaving open the possibility that over time, more appropriate or representative definitions could be found. More than this, it reflects the psychological experience of the suicidal — it is the perceptions and phenomenological experience of the individual, their assessment of the situation, their desire for escape from what (to them) is an unbearable situation, that is described (which was later termed "psychache" to further represent this experience). Furthermore, suicide is described as the *"best" solution*; this is not to say that suicide is objectively "good" in any sense, but again it represents the judgement of the individual. This definition therefore goes beyond a desire for the appearance of a scientific, methodologically sound operationalisation and in our view it bestows meaning to the word. *This* then is what we consider suicide to be.

It is necessary to refer to such "terms of reference" given the range of terminology employed in this area of research and practice, many with overlapping and confusing meanings. Below, in Table 1.1, is one proposal for the conceptualisation of suicide and suicidal behaviour as proposed by Kosky et al. (1998), which will provide the reader with some sense of this issue.

As can clearly be seen from even the briefest of summaries, the issue of definition is not an easy one. This is something which has long frustrated researchers and practitioners alike and led to the publication of a recent review article by O'Carroll et al. (1998), and the subsequent proposal of an international system of nomenclature and classification. The final section that their paper addresses is the way in which such terms and such a nomenclature might be "marketed". The general ways in which they suggest this should be done is to publish these definitions widely, to have professionals across sectors use them in everyday practice, to have journals make these definitions a requirement before papers on the topic be accepted, and to have funding agencies only issue funding to those willing to accept and use them.

Table 1.1: A Review of the Proposed Nomenclature for the Various Levels of Suicide-Related Behaviours

I. Self-injurious thoughts and behaviours
A. Risk-taking thoughts and behaviours
1. with immediate risk (e.g. motorcycling, skydiving)
2. with remote risk (e.g. smoking, sexual promiscuity)
B. Suicide-related thoughts and behaviours
1. Suicide ideation
a. Causal ideation
b. Serious ideation
(1) persistent
(2) transient
2. Suicide-related behaviours
a. Instrumental suicide-related behaviour (ISRB)
(1) Suicide threat
(a) passive (e.g. ledge-sitting)
(b) active (e.g. verbal threat, note writing)
(2) Other ISRB
(3) Accidental death associated with ISRB
b. Suicidal acts
(1) Suicide attempt
(a) with no injuries (e.g. gun fired but missed)
(b) with injuries
(2) Suicide (completed suicide)

Source: Kosky et al. (1998).

The problem with such a proposal is that such measures would unnecessarily restrict the type of work being done in the area. If we limit ourselves at this stage, when even the authors above make the point that we have not achieved sufficient understanding of the motivation, causes, etc. of suicide, then surely we are limiting the questions we ask and ultimately what we seek to know. Most importantly for us, their proposed definitions do not lend themselves to a socio-cultural approach in any form.

Although it might be a realistic possibility to work from within the definitions we already have (for there is certainly a vast selection) rather than to make additional proposals, to work from within the limits set by O'Carroll et al. is unreasonable and premature.

While an international and universally accepted definition continues to be sought, it is perhaps also of concern that the WHO definition (which appears most popular in the gathering and submitting of national statistics) makes no reference to cultural and/or temporal elements, especially at a time when many authors are coming to give these factors a central place in their examination of suicide.

In conclusion, Shneidman's definition better facilitates contemporary investigations because it allows the possibility that for different people, at different times, and in different cultures, the meaning of suicide and its very label will change. It is this flexibility and relativity that makes it attractive to a study of how temporal and cultural factors may influence suicide.

Chapter 2

Irish Suicide

Now

In Ireland now, why so many
young men kill themselves?
If the Liffey became a river of money
would it flow towards a sea of poverty?
Why do mirrors laugh at girls
looking at mirrors?
Why is a rope a hope beyond no hope?
Why does the sea invite young hearts
with happy words like
"Good night, sweet prince, good night"?

— Brendan Kennelly (2001)

Here we rely much upon Sean Spellissy's detailed account of historic and popular perspectives on suicide in Ireland, and we recommend this text to the interested reader, as we can represent but a small part of it here.

Language, Mythology and Folklore

Spellissy (1996) cites Dinneen (1927) who traced suicide back to its Irish language roots. *Anbhás* or *an-íd* were both traditionally used. *Anbhás* means a sudden and violent death and is derived from *anbha* (meaning great or terrible) and *bás* (death). Thus, *Thug sé anbhás air féin* (he took a sudden and violent death upon himself) or, in English, he committed suicide. The alternative is *an-íd* or *anaoid* to mean a tragic fate, mutilation, ill-treatment or death. Dinneen believed that all were derived from *oidheadh*, the act of slaying, doom, fate or the tragedy one deserves. *Thug sé an-íd air féin* (he took a tragic fate on himself).

Suicide in the formal and judicial sense was not a word that was officially used in Ireland for many years, as it remained a criminal offence until the Criminal Law (Suicide) Act of 1993. Prior to this, the Coroner's Act (1962) determined, in sections 30 and 31, the following:

> Section 30: Questions of civil or criminal liability shall not be considered or investigated at an inquest and accordingly every inquest shall be confined to ascertaining the identity of the person in relation to whose death the inquest is being held and how, when and where the death occurred and . . .
>
> Section 31(1): Neither the verdict nor any rider to the verdict at an inquest shall contain a censure or exoneration of any person; and 31(2): Notwithstanding anything contained in subsection (1) of this section, recommendations of a general character designed to prevent further fatalities may be appended to the verdict at any inquest.

For as long as suicide remained a criminal offence, passing the judgment of death by suicide had many unwanted consequences, not least of which was that the deceased individual would have the element of criminality attached to their final living act and their family would suffer additional and unnecessary shame and stigma. Coroners were unwilling to do this, as it was seen as being outside the remit of their professional obligation. While it has been argued that this practice resulted in Ireland having unreliable records of the actual suicide rate, more recent authors such as Kelleher et al. (1996) make the point that figures over the last decade are reliable and representative of a true estimation of Irish suicide, an issue to which we will later return.

In addition to this, Spellissy (1996) offers up an interesting and somewhat alternative view on why suicide was held as a criminal act for so long. According to a 1791 Act, post-execution dissection of the bodies of criminals was allowed, with the additional provision in the Anatomy Act (1832) providing for the adequate supply of cadavers for teaching purposes to all medical institutions. While Spellissy does not present any direct evidence that the bodies of suicides were used in this manner, there is no reason to suspect that they were not, given that people who died from suicide were classed as criminals. This activity is also known to have been a lucrative one, with records of a Mrs Wyse Power (1907) noting that 40 unclaimed bodies sent to the various medical schools over a period of a month earned the doctor in question twenty-five pence and the delivery porter twelve and a half pence per corpse. As with the official position of the Church, mentioned in Chapter 1, it appears that medical attitudes towards suicide and practices surrounding the act, were both influenced by social factors beyond the victim's demise.

While it may have been the case that for the purposes of the Coroner's Court individuals were not known to have completed the act of suicide, Irish mythology and folklore is replete with examples of suicide, and this tells us that suicide was embedded within the cultural construction of people's social lives:

> Deirdre of the Sorrows was the daughter of a story-teller named Feighlimidh. She was reared in seclusion after Cathnadh the druid prophesied that she would be the cause of great slaughter amongst the men of Ulster. She fell in love with Naoise, one of the three sons of Usna, although Conor MacNeasa, the King of Ulster, had declared he would marry her himself. She eloped with Naoise and his brothers but Conor had the fugitives pursued throughout the length and breadth of Ireland. The sons of Usna eluded capture and eventually sought refuge as mercenaries in Scotland. The King of Scotland, however, became inflamed with Deirdre's beauty and jealous of Naoise, and the four fugitives had to flee his court. They found safety in a remote Scottish glen or island until three notable Ulster warriors persuaded them to return to Ireland . . . Deirdre was forced to live with Conor for a year but she succeeded in killing herself before he could give her to another hated enemy . . . She committed suicide by dashing her head against a huge rock in a manoeuvre known as "warrior's salmon leap" (Spellissy, 1996, p. 22).

This tale presents suicide as the "rational" option in response to Deirdre's life-situation, seen neither as sin nor crime. Deirdre is not presented as a "madwoman" incapable of lucidly choosing a fate, but as someone who perceives suicide as the "best solution". In this sense, Deirdre's actions can be seen to meet Shneidman's criteria for suicide (see Chapter 1).

> *Grian* or *Gile Gréine*, thought to be from *Tuatha Dé Danann* (the Otherworld of Celtic mythology) but born of a mortal on a sunbeam, was a famous beauty. However, when she learned of her origins, she is said to have become depressed and decided to end her life in a lake (now called Lough Graney) (Spellissy, 1996).

Although coming from ancient tales, the motives for Grian's act of self-destruction are familiar to readers of today, with what Shneidman called "psychache" being understandable to people across ages. Not only does this testify to the storytelling talent of the people who told and re-told these tales, but it may also be seen to attest to the enduring aspects of the human condition that can lead one to the point of suicide. Our world may have changed but our humanity has not.

Finally, *Cúchulainn* (one of Ulster's greatest and best-known heroes) died in battle. When his body was recovered, his widow Emer asked Conall of the Battles, who had avenged his death, that a wide grave be dug. When this was done, Emer climbed into the grave beside the body of her husband, kissed him on the lips and willed herself to die. She could not envisage life without him and thought that he might be in need of her passion and courage in the Otherworld, with the *Sidhe* (fairy-folk) not being enough to guide him. Her death is presented as the act of a dutiful wife (Spellissy, 1996).

These examples refer to female characters. It is important to note that male characters were seen as equally capable of the act, although there were additional complications in defining male suicide. There existed certain prohibitions on the acts of warriors being classed as suicide — the Irish *geas*, understood as a magical taboo or spell of obligation prevented the warrior carrying out certain behaviour on pain of death or misfortune, with the right of imposing the *geas* falling to a woman (Spellissy, 1996). If a warrior carried out an action in order to meet the obligations of a *geas* but which he also knew would result in his own death, he was not thought to have committed suicide but behaved honourably and in keeping with traditional custom.

Another way in which suicide entered into Irish folklore was through the belief that anyone born on Whit Sunday would cause death or die a sudden and violent death (the latter of which, Spellissy argues, sounds very much like the traditional definition of a suicide). The only way to prevent the fulfilment of this prophecy was to have the *Cíncgíseach* or Pentecostal-born kill another creature. Traditionally, this was done by placing live insects in the hand of the infant and closing their hand over until the insects had died, thus preventing the tragic outcome. Through these few examples, we can see that even from ancient times the role of social and cultural mores in the determination and understanding of suicide was substantial.

The Unconfessed Sin and Fasting upon the Enemy . . .

Spellissy (1996) presents the anecdote of an elderly mission priest who made something of a wager with his Donegal congregation. The priest said that he was incapable of being shocked or embarrassed as there was no sin that had not been confessed to him during the course of his life-long vocation. He promised a reward of ten pounds to anyone who could name a sin that had never been confessed to him. This wager did not appear to be much of a gamble, until one of the congregation piped up, "What about suicide, father?"

As has been seen, the Catholic Church's position on suicide is long-established and well-known; however, people who killed themselves were still buried (albeit in an alternative manner) with certain cultural practices surrounding this rite. It is important to examine these in order to gain some understanding of the way in which Irish people traditionally dealt with the difficult situation of mourning their dead within a prohibitive context.

Suicides were buried in *killeens* or *kyles*, marked on maps as "children's or disused burial grounds" and which remained in existence up to the 1950s and 1960s. These were the same places that were reserved for the burial of unbaptised babies and children. The reason for this was that the soul of the deceased was believed to exist in a state of *limbo* if death occurred before baptism could take place. This was common in an era when women who had just given birth (seen almost as impure) had to be *churched* before they could re-enter the general Catholic community. Such ceremonies were usually carried out between sunset and sunrise. In addition to the burial of children and suicides, these burial sites were also the final resting place of dwarves, Jews, peddlers and paupers, making clear the status that was generally afforded to suicidal deaths at this time. A clear example of the punitive and judgemental way in which such deaths were viewed comes from practices in the area of County Down where it was said that those who had committed suicide were condemned to re-enact the method of their death for eternity (Spellissy, 1996).

It was also known for suicides to be buried at a crossroads. Kelleher (1996) suggests that this served two purposes: the first, that the evil thought to have caused the suicide would be "confused" by such a placement of the body, thus making it unable to return to the town/village and cause another similar death; and secondly, that the crossroads was a public rather than a private domain, thus the shame was not placed on any one individual or group of individuals.

Another practice commonly associated with this time was the placement of a wooden stake through the heart of someone who had killed themselves, in order to drive out the perceived "evil spirits" responsible for them having carried out such a heinous act. Bowers (1994) raises the possibility that this provided the inspiration for Bram Stoker's *Dracula*, as Stoker is known to have passed a suicide plot at Ballybough cemetery on his way to work each day. This practice was formally banned in 1882 under the Internments (*felo de se*) Act, which stated that:

> it shall not be lawful for any coroner or other officer having authority to hold inquests to issue any warrant or other process directing the internment of the remains of persons against whom a finding of *felo de se*[1] shall be had in any public highway or with any stake being driven through the body of such person.

While this is certainly a negative view of both suicides and unbaptised children (who generally shared the same status), more

---

[1] *Felo de se*, as a term, has in interesting history. Translated literally, it means "he who kills" and was used as a legal term but was unique in that its definition related to the criminal rather than the crime. So, even in legal usage, value judgements were passed on the nature of suicide and its definition.

positive beliefs are know to have been held elsewhere. The folklore of Russia, Scotland and parts of Ireland (e.g. Donegal and Galway) argued that the souls of those so deceased animated the bodies of elves, giving out the light known as Wil O' the Wisp and that they were entrusted with the task of bringing the souls of the newly dead to the gates of heaven (O'Donoghue, 1894).

"Fasting upon the enemy" is another way in which suicide made its way into the Irish psyche. The complaining individual would camp on the doorstep of the defendant (or individual who was held responsible for the perceived wrong) until such time as the problem was remedied or the complainant died (Spellissy, 1996). Traditional Ireland held hospitality in such high regard that this was seen as the ultimate countermeasure. Not only did the defendant have to endure the unwelcome guest, but, in the event of their death, the defendant was responsible for the compensation of their family. Kelly (1988) makes the point that hunger strike is not to be seen as the modern equivalent of the traditional fasting against the enemy. However, if one views both as exerting moral and socio-cultural pressure to a desired end, they may be seen to share certain elements.

John Daly (1846–1916), leader of the Irish Republican Brotherhood, is noted as the first to have used hunger strike against the British. He was arrested for carrying explosives and sentenced to life imprisonment in Birkenhead on 11 April 1884. He was released having served twelve and a half years. Later, political movements such as that of the Suffragettes also adopted this technique, as did some famous Republicans who were imprisoned such as Thomas Ashe (the first Republican hunger striker to die). Interestingly, Kelleher (1996) makes the point that, even in more modern times, self-starvation could be presented as an acceptable form of death. Members of the IRA who were imprisoned as a result of their activities in the "fight for freedom" argued that they should be afforded special status while interned (for want of a better term, they presented themselves as prisoners of war, thus warranting special consideration). When the British Government arbitrarily restricted this special status category to those convicted after 1 March 1976, the most unremitting series of hunger strikes in Irish history began. Bobby Sands died on 5 May 1981 following 66 days of fasting, the first of ten men who ended their lives in this manner. In the earlier case of Terence MacSwiney, the staunchly Roman Catholic de Valera encouraged the fast, even if it resulted in his death. Furthermore, the Catholic Church's inconsistent approach to suicide can be seen in the MacSwiney case, as he was honoured with a full Catholic burial in the presence of two bishops and some four hundred clergymen, despite his mode of death. On this basis, we see once again that a great deal of context (and in the case of the traditional Church, hypocrisy) surrounds suicide, with even religious biases being overcome to achieve socio-political goals, in certain situations.

SUICIDE IN CONTEMPORARY IRELAND

Today, suicides are buried within graveyards and hunger strikes are a less prominent feature of Irish politics. Myths regarding Deirdre and Cúchulainn form part of the school curriculum and are not taught as part of a suicide prevention programme, but as part of Irish cultural heritage. Suicide has, nonetheless, become a very real feature of modern Ireland, with the statistics becoming no less startling or concerning as they become more familiar.

In the first six months of 2001, 43 people between the ages of 15 and 24 took their own lives (CSO).[2] In the previous year, the annual total came to 104 for this same age group (see Chapter 5 for additional information). When the gender ratio for youth suicide (classed throughout this text as that occurring between 15 and 24 years) was last considered, it had reached a high of seven male suicides to every one female (Kelleher, 1998) and, when considered at a county-by-county level, reached its highest ratio of 10:1 in 2000 in the South Eastern Health Board Area (IAS, 2000). When the National Task Force on Suicide (1998) presented their final report, it was estimated that the ultimate financial cost of deaths by suicide for the period 1991–94 reached £75,600,000. This sum was reached by applying a statistical formula from a similar study in the United States and taking into account loss of economic productivity due to the deaths of young, productive members of society. While it is

---

[2] Personal communication with Central Statistics Officer.

useful in some respects to see the economic impact of suicide, the human cost is immeasurable. Nevertheless, as we have seen in both personal and economic terms, Ireland is indeed experiencing a considerable suicide problem.

There exists an argument that in order to reduce these suicide rates, access to means should be restricted. This is known as the *availability hypothesis*. This is a feature of the newly released Best Practice Guidelines for Suicide Prevention in Irish schools (Irish Association of Suicidology and National Suicide Review Group, 2002), which states that hanging is the most common means of suicide in Ireland in both males and females under the age of 25 (see Figure 2.1). This counters the notion that females generally use less violent methods and, given the difficulty in restricting access to the necessary elements for hanging, the prevention difficulties when following the access restriction model or availability hypothesis are clear.

Drowning is the next most common means and, while the National Taskforce Report (1998) proposed the widespread implementation of swimming lessons, this is also a difficult area, as access to water cannot reasonably be restricted. Firearms are most frequently used by males in the 15–24 year age bracket, with evidence from international studies showing a positive effect in restricting the ease of availability of this method (Hawton, Fagg, Simkin, Harriss and Malmberg, 1998). An important point here however is that some substitution of means has been reported; in other words, for some people at least, if a completed suicide is intended, any means necessary will be employed.

Self-poisoning, although present in the general perception of suicide, is a less common method in the 15–24 year age bracket. European research has shown this to be the preferred method for parasuicidal acts, not resulting in death. UK studies recorded a second annual decrease in 1998 in the proportion of non-fatal overdoses involving paracetamol, since the effort to reduce pack sizes and the introduction of blister packs (Irish Association of Suicidology and National Suicide Review Group, 2002). In Ireland, the National Task Force and the Irish Association of Suicidology have made similar recommendations with the restriction of sale and supply in shops and chemists having become a regulation since 1 October 2001.

Figure 2.1: Method of Suicide, 1996–2000

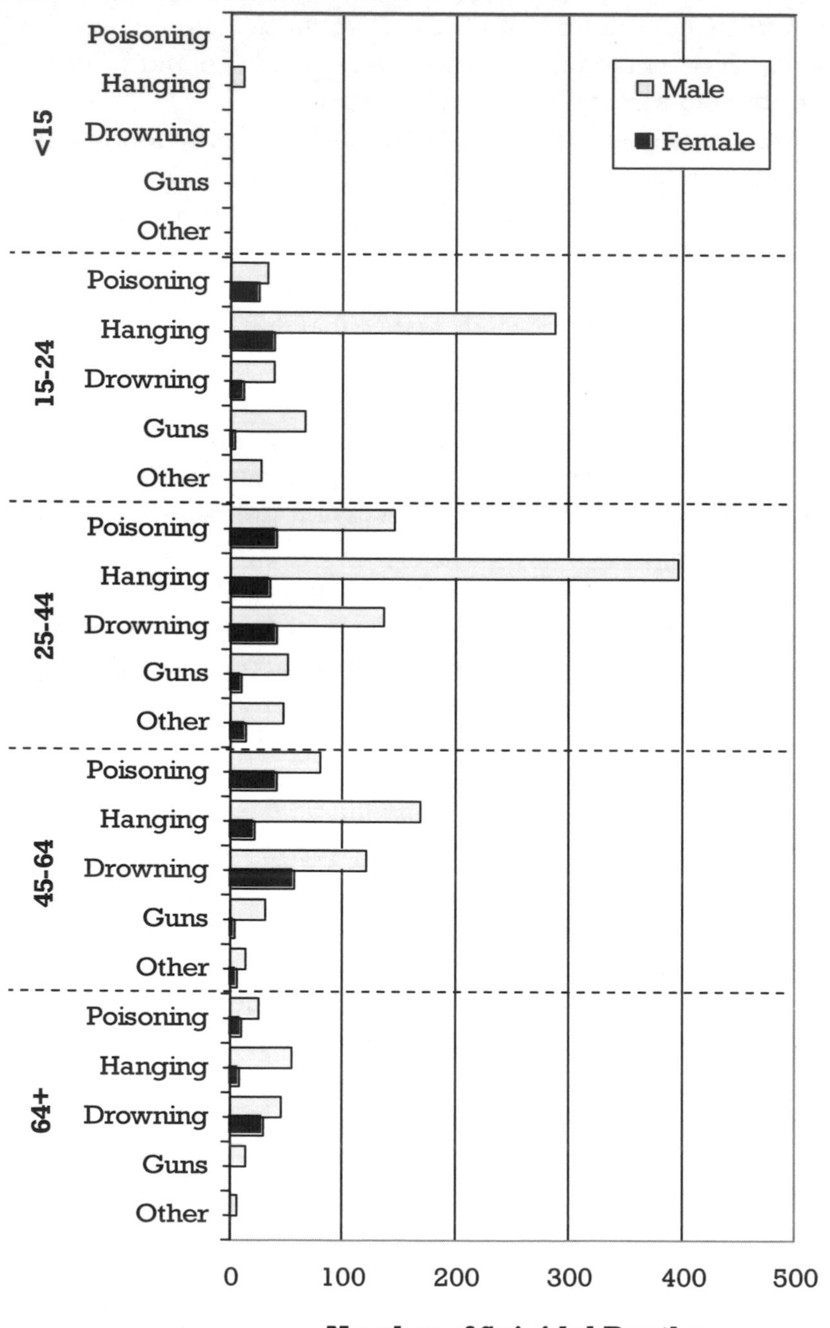

Source: Central Statistics Office.

While the availability hypothesis is common in suicide prevention plans, with authors such as Williams and Pollock (2000) asserting that the availability of means may be enough to facilitate an attempt by an impulsive at-risk individual, there are some noted difficulties with it. Pounder (1991), in an examination of the Scottish increase in young male suicide, found that the observed rise was mostly attributable to the use of hanging and carbon monoxide poisoning. Both the acceptability and availability of these methods (to people contemplating suicide) was examined and the conclusion reached that the "acceptance" of hanging may have followed on from the cessation of judicial hanging in Scottish Law from 1965. Furthermore, these methods are presented as being age-specific, making the point that while the restriction of access to means may indeed be a useful approach, it does not necessarily hold across all age groups and so is to be considered more critically in terms of its value as a general preventative measure. In a similar vein, Beautrais (2000) presented almost identical findings from an Australian sample where it was seen that suicide had increased most notably among young males with preferred methods being hanging and, to a lesser extent, carbon monoxide poisoning. Therefore, these particular methods, which do not readily lend themselves to the approach of reducing their availability, appear to be shared across nations in this age group.

When discussing Irish suicide research, it would indeed be remiss to fail to mention Dr Michael J. Kelleher, founder of the National Suicide Review Group, and one of the best-known Irish writers on the topic of suicide. His book *Suicide and the Irish*, published in 1996, covers a range of topics and although it appears to present a somewhat traditional view of Irish life and the more recent changes, some of his points resonate with our own approach.

One of the crucial points he tackles concerns the recent increase in Irish suicides. While some ask if this is a *real* increase, or merely the effect of more accurate reporting, Kelleher (among others) has argued that while there were certainly issues surrounding the official statistics for many years, not only are recent figures accurate (inasmuch as possible) but that the increase observed *is indeed real*. An interesting way in which he makes this point is to examine the rate of suicide in the Irish abroad. While these rates were higher than those of the Irish in Ireland, they were on the whole comparatively low (as was the Irish rate when considered at an international level), he claims. This has not remained the case as we have seen with the increasing figures. One element of hope, however, can be inferred from the point that Kelleher makes on what was once a protective culture within our island: those elements that guarded against suicide were brought with those who emigrated (thus helping to keep the emigrant rate of suicide low) and so, some features of Irish culture in the past offered a "buffer" against suicide. The very fact that he mentions culture is significant and certainly progressive, as he moves beyond traditional individualised and reductionist medical conceptualisations of suicide: from the "I" to the "we", making suicide everyone's concern.

If this was the case once, then perhaps it is also possible for the future. This statement is not to be seen as a simplistic reduction. Suicide prevention is no easy matter (as we will see when the issue is considered in greater detail in Chapter 6) but this offers a more positive view than those who will reflect a fatalistic position with the statement that suicide cannot be prevented.

Kelleher also asserts that while figures for youth cancer, youth suicide and road traffic accidents are frequently compared (and share the top three places for causes of youth death), suicide may be seen to have more in common with road deaths than with cancer. There is no element of choice in cancer; it is a medical condition which, although treatable in certain forms, is something that the individual does not generally "choose" for themselves (arguments regarding smoking aside). Road traffic deaths, in contrast, often reflect the consequences of human error or misjudgement and in this sense are preventable at some level (clearly excluding those tragic deaths that can only be seen as the result of chance). If we see suicide as preventable and approach the issue with this in mind, we are surely in a better position to protect our youth and provide them with a sense of hope for the future — a feature of mental health education that can only be positive.

In this chapter, suicide has been considered from its presence in traditional Celtic tales, to the Republican hunger-strikers of the 1970s and early 1980s, to more modern research and commentary. It was our aim to illustrate that although Ireland's high suicide rate is relatively new, suicide has long been a feature of our existence, our psyche, our culture. In the next chapter, we will look more closely at this last aspect — culture — and examine the way in which it might be included in modern examinations of suicide.

Chapter 3

WHY CULTURE?

Culture is always something that was,
Something pedants can measure,
Skull of bard, thigh of chief,
Depth of dried-up river.
Shall we be thus for ever?
Shall we be thus for ever?

— Patrick Kavanagh (from "Memory of Brother Michael")

> Culture is the nutrient medium within which the organism is cultivated. Suicidality grows, as well, when that culture is pathological . . . Suicidal behaviour can be designed to protect, to rescue the self from otherwise certain annihilation (Berman, 1997, p. 6).

Western psychology and psychiatry, by focusing their attention on the individual, came to see suicide as the deviant act of a disturbed, dysfunctional or ill mind. Suicide thus became both individualised and pathologised. Culture, from this stance, was either not included or was included in only the most superficial of ways, adopting what is known as a "transport and test" approach. David Lester, in particular, is renowned for this and, while a cross-cultural comparison of suicide rates facilitates the establishment of an international database on the phenomenon, and related issues in diverse populations, it continues to neglect culture at a more fundamental level. We argue that culture — that which organises and shapes our understanding of reality, the way we interact with the world and those in it, and that which gives meaning to our lives (Gergen and Gergen, 1996) — is a central facet of suicide. Having shown how the meaning of suicide has changed through different epochs, we now briefly illustrate how it also differs across contemporary cultural contexts.

In essence, the cultural perspective emphasises that different social groupings create different social contexts in which suicide may occur. O'Connor (2001) also addressed this issue by asking: Is suicide to be seen as the result of a bad apple or a rotten barrel? The "bad apple" approach is characteristic of traditional psychology and psychiatry where suicide is seen as "belonging" to the person — the "I". Not only does this restrict the type of research questions we can ask (as it precludes questioning the role of society at a broader level) but it also impedes the way research findings may be taken up. If schools and community groups see suicide as existing only in the mentally ill population, they may be reluctant to put into place education and prevention measures. This is something that has to be overcome if the issue of youth suicide, specifically, is to be adequately addressed, leading O'Connor to the point that suicide would better be seen as a continuum of behaviours which any one of us could adopt given the "right" circumstances.

The second approach, the "rotten barrel", more closely approximates the stance adopted by traditional sociology (and contemporary critical psychology) and looks to the broader socio-cultural world for explanation and understanding. Curran (1987) makes a statement which puts this point into clearer focus, stating that youth suicide is "a monstrous coupling of two incompatible facts, youth and death, which throws our sense of *meaning and order* into chaos" (p. 280, italics added). As soon as you start to consider meaning and order, the patterning of life, you are referring to culture. Different cultures create different meanings and different orders (MacLachlan, 2001).

To illustrate this point, we now briefly review suicide in some other contemporary cultural settings. When multicultural perspectives on suicide are examined, it becomes clear that culture may act either as a *protective factor* or as one that increases risk in already vulnerable groups — a *facilitating factor*. It is important to emphasise that culture and national boundaries are not the same. For instance, we are now fond of talking about different "traditions" within Northern Ireland and of increasingly recognising that the Republic is not mono-cultural (nor has it ever been). In the United States, there are clearly many different cultural groups, both in terms of First Nations groups ("native" North Americans — often referred to, due to a navigational error, by the complete misnomer "Indians") and the many immigrant groups, including descendants of African "slaves" and more contemporary cheap labour from poorer countries, near and far.

Range et al. (1999) examine various ethnic groups within the United States with regard to the role played by factors such as values, attitudes, world views, religion, traditional belief, family and acculturation. Range et al. (1999) also emphasise the important distinction between the constructs of race and ethnicity. *Race* is traditionally an anthropological term that has historically referred to a common set of physical characteristics. Anthropologists distinguished between three broad "races"; Negroid, Mongoloid and Caucasian, on the basis of presumed genetic differences. However, the term "race" holds little positive value today as it is now recognised by most people (including anthropologists) to be a socio-political construct which may facilitate discriminatory social hierarchies and further prejudice. Furthermore, it is also recognised that the genetic variation within these so-called "races" is greater than between them, for many characteristics (MacLachlan, 1997). Thus the term "race", socio-political considerations aside, has little biological value. It is widely held that the term "ethnic group" is to be preferred. Range et al. (1999) argue that this is a multidimensional construct that refers to a group of people with a common origin and shared or common cultural elements. This latter view is especially appropriate when considering multiculturalism.

To emphasis our distinction between national boundaries and the ethnic diversity within these, we will begin by considering two ethnic groups in the United States who occupy opposite extremes in that country's statistics of suicide. One has the highest rate of suicide, while the other has the lowest, yet they are both minority groups, marginalised by "mainstream" US society. We are particularly interested to see what it is about their different cultural experiences that create different "possibilities" for suicide.

African-American Culture

Suicide is the only condition in which the African-American population exhibit lower rates than their European-American counterparts (Allen and Farley, 1986) in spite of the fact that this group are often economically and socially disadvantaged. This said, within African-Americans there is a male to female ratio of approximately four to one, with the greatest at-risk periods being between the ages of 25 and 34 years, and the most common case of suicide being that of young men using a gun, or some other high-lethality means. Thus, while this group as a whole has lower levels of suicide than, for instance, Anglo-Americans, the same gender-based trend is seen.

Another noteworthy finding is that a clear relationship is seen to exist between accidental death, homicide and suicide, with one proposed explanation being that, due to stereotypic expectations, African-Americans may be more likely to have negative (or even fatal) encounters with the police, thus adding to the high rate of death (Gibbs, 1988). Whether this explanation is accepted or not, suicidal behaviour in the African-American population is surrounded by distinct socio-cultural, political and economic issues. That mental health status is not the only factor considered (as it so often is with other groups) and that these other elements may be more salient, again, makes it noteworthy.

African-American culture may serve to protect against suicide in several ways. Early et al. (1993) assert that religion in this group provides steadfast support to families given the level of integration which members experience. In addition, suicide is seen as an "unpardonable sin" alien not only to their religion but also to African-Americans on the whole. Further to this, African-Americans are also more likely than those of European extraction to live in multigenerational groupings, and this offers the possibility of elderly suicide being reduced, since elderly people can feel that they continue to make a valuable and meaningful contribution to their family and their community.

When the clinical implications for the African-American population are considered, Range et al. (1999) make the point that some move away from traditional Western individualised psychological approaches should be made, and that the extended family ought to be included in interventions.

Native American Culture

Moving on to consider Native American groups (or "First Nations", i.e. "we were here first") one of the most striking features of these groups is the level of poverty and alcohol dependence encountered. Both of these problems are recognised as independent risk factors for suicide, which is higher in this group than for any other on mainland North America, especially in the 15–24-year-old category (EchoHawk, 1997).

One of the main concerns with regard to the suicide rate of the various Native American groups is the impact the process of acculturation has had. The theory of acculturation will be dealt with shortly; for now, suffice it to say that acculturation refers to the way in which individuals relate to, in terms of their attitudes and behaviours, and come to exist within, a cultural context that may not be the same as the socio-cultural context into which they were socialised.

When faced with the problems of tribal relocation and deregulation of tribal life, maladaptive forms of coping have been observed; including alcohol dependence. Furthermore, in the absence of a formal rite of passage (further reflecting imposed changes on the structure of tribal life) signalling the move from childhood to adolescence, consumption of alcohol may begin at very early ages, with Range et al. (1999) noting that, in some tribes, children as young as six have been seen to participate in tribal drinking sessions. Furthermore, some self-reports suggest that males in particular drink with the specific intention of becoming intoxicated with alcohol being used as a means of escape and a form of psychological analgesic (ibid.).

Despite the apparently clear links between substance use and suicidal behaviour, Novins et al. (1999) assert that a more complex view of this relationship is needed if a more accurate picture is to be obtained. In comparing the Pueblo, Southwest and Northwest tribal groups (specific names were not mentioned in the study for reasons of confidentiality) the best explanation of the link between substance use (e.g. alcohol) and suicide was that it made people more likely to act on suicidal thoughts. In short, alcohol does not *cause* people to have suicidal thoughts or behave in a suicidal manner, but for those who already hold such thoughts, the consumption of alcohol may make them more likely to act (that is, it may reduce inhibition for suicide). If, as we have seen, alcohol is used as a form of coping, this information points to the need for education on healthier and more adaptive coping behaviours so that when faced with problems or stressors, individuals do not engage in a behaviour (in this case, drinking) which may make them more likely to end their lives.

Approximately one-third of Native Americans live on reservations, another third live in urban settings with the remaining third living between reservation and urban areas. When suicide is considered among the tribes, reports range from 150 per 100,000 to zero per 100,000, depending on the tribe and source of statistics. The male to female ratio has been recorded at a high of 12:1, with lethal means being used frequently by males (55.2 per cent of male suicides in this group are as a result of use of firearms with a further 40 per cent adopting the method of hanging). Reflecting this, Range et al. (1999) offer the typical profile of a Native American suicide as being that of a young, single male who kills himself at home with a firearm following a drinking session. Further to this, when three tribes (the Navajo, Apache and Pueblos) were compared, it was the Apache who were seen to have the highest rate of suicide and the lowest level of intra-tribal (i.e. within their own tribe) social integration, thus further pointing to the role of social and cultural factors in the experience of suicide.

When the role of culture is considered in connection with suicide, traditional tribal structure is presented as key. EchoHawk (1997) offers us a view of tribal structure as circular, divided into seven parts (the example being drawn from the Otoe-Missouria Tribe of Oklahoma) representing the clans of the tribe. Within each clan is a further subdivision by biological relationship, although all members of the clan are seen to be related irrespective of formal biological links. Somewhat paradoxical to Western ears is the fundamental notion that it was by diversity and subdivision that cohesiveness and interdependence were promoted and maintained. For example, each clan would have a healer skilled to deal with one aspect of health (setting broken bones, haemorrhaging, curing sick children, healing eye injuries or diseases or mental illness), but no clan would have a healer skilled to deal with all complaints. Thus, while the position of healer was shared across groups, the particular specialty was unique. In this way, mutual recognition, respect and interdependence could occur. This same structure was seen in the areas of education, moral upbringing and craftsmanship, with general cohesiveness maintained by relationships, status and roles.

Elements of acculturation such as Western education (by Mission schools or boarding schools; see Berry, 1969), religious conversion, legislation, language barriers and being moved from native lands to reservations, can all be seen to have contributed to the suicide problem. If a culture orders and gives meaning to life experiences, the dismantling of that culture may result in a disordered and personally meaningless world. Traditional safeguards that protected against suicide, such as the previously mentioned interdependence, clear role-orientation and traditional tribal structure, are no longer typical. In contrast, modern tribal structure is characterised by chaotic family structures, divorce, alcoholism and child neglect, meaning that Native American cultures (as they are today) play a more negative role than before and in this way are seen to be linked to suicide (EchoHawk, 1997).

On this latter point of modern tribal culture, six variables in particular have been recognised as being of importance in predicting the likelihood of suicide in Native American peoples:

- Having more than one significant caretaker prior to age 15;
- Primary caretakers with numerous arrests;
- Two or more losses by divorce or desertion during childhood;
- Being arrested by age 15;
- One or more arrests in the twelve months prior to death; and
- Attendance at a boarding school before ninth grade (Dizmang, Watson, May and Bopp, 1974).

Thus, by the process of culture change and the resultant effects of acculturation, what was once a unique and strong culture is now plagued by suicide and, while EchoHawk offers some hope for the future (for example, Native American tribes now have the opportunity to implement self-run, community-based health interventions) much effort will be needed if the protective elements are to be returned to this culture. In short, and in EchoHawk's own words, "indigenous clients must be allowed to grieve and talk about their feelings of historical trauma, alienation and poor sense of identity" (p. 66) if the positive culture of the past is to be reclaimed, re-established and re-awakened.

We will return to a consideration of how mental health can be enhanced and suicide prevented among North American First Nations, when we look to achieving the same in Irish society in our final chapter. There are clearly numerous cultures and contrasting constructions of suicide and in the interests of brevity we can consider very few. We think, however, that there are sufficient similarities — at least superficially — between Ireland and New Zealand/Aotearoa to consider, in particular, the Maori culture in some detail.

Aotearoa's Maori Culture[1]

Of the 23 OECD (Organisation for Economic Cooperation and Development) countries that returned statistics on youth suicide, New Zealand ranks first for suicides in males in the 15–24 years age bracket. Equivalent UNICEF data from 32 societies places New Zealand third in terms of male suicide (15–24 years) and eighth highest for female suicides (15–24 years). Beautrais (2000) shows that New Zealand has experienced a steady increase in the rate of youth suicide over the period 1977–96 from 20.3 per 100,000 to 39.5 per 100,000. (It is important to note that during this same period, female rates of suicide remained steady, as is the general international pattern in nations dominated by male suicide.) In New Zealand and Ireland, certain shared characteristics of youth suicide are to be seen. Of the

---

[1] Aotearoa is the Maori name for New Zealand and is becoming increasingly used in both official and colloquial contexts.

100 nations reporting suicide statistics to the World Health Organisation (2002) New Zealand ranked twenty-third and Ireland twenty-fourth in terms of the overall rate of male suicide. The one area where greatest difference is to be found is in the gender ratio of youth suicides. While Ireland ranks first of 32 surveyed nations for male to female ratio for this age group (eleven male suicides for every one female suicide), New Zealand exhibited a lower ratio of six male suicides for every one female suicide (Office of the Commissioner for Children, 1996).

Langford et al. (1998) have considered the possible cultural and social mediators of suicide in terms of the historical and socio-cultural development of New Zealand/Aotearoa. The question that arises is why (in much the same way as Ireland) a relatively affluent, economically secure, historically socially supportive nation, has such high levels of youth suicide.

Of the 3.6 million people of New Zealand, 400,000 are Maori. They are therefore considered to be a minority group. This minority status is also associated with colonial oppression, land loss, low socioeconomic status and generally poor health. Following World War II, there was a massive shift from rural to urban settings, which was seen to affect the Maori role in society, especially that of women (Schwimmer, 1968).

Mythological literature may be examined in order to more clearly examine the traditional Maori national character and the impact culture change has had upon it. These depictions are replete with (presumed) strong male characteristics such as stoicism, dourness, endurance, not complaining, ironic good humour, fashioning with one's hands, hiding tender emotions etc. This was the clear male role which developed into an icon (and remains so) of the "good keen man". Phillips (1996) argues that this icon may still be seen in the way in which sporting heroes are portrayed and through what appears to be almost a national attitude of "John Henryism" (James, Hartnett, and Kalsbeek, 1983); such that there exists a belief that anything can be achieved and the environment controlled if you work hard enough. Such individuation of belief in the nature of success and failure has clear implications — for example, in the experience of depression — if "I" as an individual believe that "I" am personally responsible for those elements in my world that lead to success, then surely "I" must also take responsibility for any failure I experience. Thus, the "I" after experiencing enough perceived, personal failures must surely be vulnerable to a sense of hopelessness. In this way, cultural socialisation may predispose individuals to hopelessness, given a certain pattern of outcomes.

In addition to this, Maori men experience a pervasive sense of relative disadvantage. While societal development has allowed Paheka (White) men to experience a certain status and associated benefits, Maori men do not share in this, although they are aware of the situation of their Paheka counterparts.

This may be linked to suicide under what Barber (2001) terms the "relative misery hypothesis". Unlike Durkheim's theory on the link between socio-cultural factors and suicide, which argued that as a society develops it becomes less integrated and offers a reduced level of cohesion to its members, Barber argues that quite a different mechanism is at work. What is important in this theory is the relative misery of young men especially, who in the presence of societal development and increased prosperity and/or success, make upwards social comparisons (e.g. "look what they have that I do not") with their counterparts, thus magnifying their relative unhappiness and making an already vulnerable group more susceptible to suicidal behaviours. While Barber has not extended this theory to Maori populations, it is reasonable to suggest that this recognised mechanism could be at work.

Historically, there has been a low suicide rate among the Maori and an examination of the underlying cultural construction is therefore important to understand. Death in the Maori language is translated as *mate*. There is no specific translation for *suicide* as English speakers would understand it, with the closest approximation being the word *whakamomori* which does not imply death directly but a loss of alternatives so overwhelming that death is the result. The root of the word *mori* means distress, helplessness, unfulfilled desire, broken attachment etc., perhaps linguistically representing a more holistic view which more accurately reflects the psychological experience we know to often precede suicide.

In traditional Maori culture, there are recognised circumstances in which self-inflicted death is seen as "acceptable".

Among these is the sudden loss of some significant other, intolerable loss of status, overwhelming insult, personal failure to perform in some valued domain or a belief that some powerful magic has been performed against the person. Maori morality is determined by elements such as honour, respect, status, politically imposed restrictions and supernatural events.

In general, suicidal behaviour is based on *shame* with a traditional source of motivation more akin to Japanese suicide than suicide in the West. While Western suicide has traditionally been motivated by *guilt*, Japanese suicide has been observed to be more shame-based (Ryan, 1985) with a similar pattern outlined above in the Maori culture. It is important to state that we are *not* arguing that Japan has a disproportionately high rate of suicide. Indeed Takahashi (1997) asserts that the Japanese rate may be placed central to European rates, occupying neither the highest nor the lowest position. What is of interest, however, given our cultural analysis, are the cultural differences in suicidal motivation. The primary difference relates to Western suicide being guilt-based suicide, while Japanese suicidal behaviour is motivated by a feeling that one's behaviour is so dishonourable that to continue to live would bring great and unbearable shame to one's family. In addition, Japanese culture is said to be characterised by elements of monism, groupism, selflessness, faith and loyalty (Iga, 1986). Therefore, it is better to take one's own life than to harm one's family and loved ones. In this way, Maori suicide may have more in common with Japanese cultural values than those of the West.

Death is seen as a natural part of life (with no great fear or dread attached to it). There exists a folktale that life emerged from the primal ancestral light which was warm and nurturing, and that death is a return to this. There is no concept of hell or punishment as in Roman Catholicism, for example. In death one does not escape the concerns of life, or indeed contact with family. Dead ancestors play a very important role in Maori life and may be evoked at any time to help the living. The newly dead person has to answer to the ancestors and account for their deeds. In this sense, a wrongful suicide would have to be accounted for, which also acts as a deterrent. Thus death is not seen as an escape and, as such, this begs the question, "What would the point of suicide be?" Langford et al. (1998) argue that this set of beliefs may have contributed to the historically low suicide rate of the Maori culture.

Another very important part of the traditional Maori culture was the concept of family or *whanau*, which were the agents of socialisation (Ritchie and Ritchie, 1979). This was the place from which you derived your support, strength and comfort. In a rural setting, families used to live together in inter-generational groups. With post-war urbanisation, this became impossible and so there was the development of symbolic or surrogate families which maintained the tradition (Metge, 1995). During adolescence in particular, having this familial support was seen to be vital. In more modern urban settings, the surrogate family that adolescents find for themselves often come in the form of peer groups. Here, gang behaviour, criminality, drug/alcohol abuse etc. develop as this is their principal reference group. Using peer groups as *whanau* facilitates risky behaviour sooner than promoting support and secure individual development. It is stressed that this is a condition of *modern urban* Maori living. The authors argue that it is essential to look to these issues of identity and affiliation in order to further elucidate sociocultural elements of suicide. Thus, as with the Native American societies, rapid social change and the stripping of cultural icons and practices seems to have created a context in which suicidal behaviour flourished. One might well ask, "If culture is so fragile and so unresponsive to change, what good is it?"

The Functions of Culture

The U'wa (meaning intelligent people who know how to speak) are a traditional indigenous society within Colombia. Uribe Marin's (1999) account of how they have reacted to the continued diminishment of their lands is dramatic. In response to new plans for oil exploration, they have threatened to collectively commit suicide:

> To be severed from their place, to be removed from the context of the stories which they have passed down from gen-

> eration to generation, is to be killed as a people, and is, as they have made very clear, a fate worse than death (p. 43).

A formal statement by the U'wa helps explain this:

> We must care for, not maltreat, because for us it is forbidden to kill with knives, machetes or bullets. Our weapons are thought, the word, our power is wisdom. We prefer death before seeing our sacred ancestors profaned (cited in Marin, 1999).

If a culture can be so fatally possessing of the minds of its followers, then what good is it?

Ernest Becker was one of the great unnoticed intellectuals of the last century, possibly because he was hopelessly out of touch with the zeitgeist for reductionism. As an anthropologist who embraced the breadth of the social sciences, he dared to ask "big" questions about the meaning of life (see, for instance, Becker, 1968, 1971, 1973). Over the last fifteen years, a trio of experimental social psychologists and their students have developed and demonstrated the value of Terror Management Theory (TMT), based largely upon the writings of Becker (for reviews, see Solomon, Greenberg and Pyszczynski, 1991, 1998). Unfortunately, a review of either Becker's work, or of the many elegant experimental manipulations used to evaluate TMT, is beyond the scope of this chapter. However, the central premise of TMT is that our concerns about mortality play a pervasive and far-reaching role in our daily lives. The intelligence of human beings, coupled with their capacity for self-reflection, and the ability to think about the future, gives us the unique capacity to contemplate the inevitability of our own death.

Like Sigmund Freud and Otto Rank, Becker believed that humans would be paralysed to inaction and abject terror if they were to continually contemplate their vulnerability and mortality. Thus cultural worldviews evolved and these were "humanly created beliefs about the nature of reality shared by groups of people that served (at least in part) to manage the terror engendered by the uniquely human awareness of death" (Solomon et al., 1998, p. 12). The vision of reality created by cultural worldviews, it is argued, help to manage existential terror by answering universal cosmological questions: "Who am I? What should I do? What will happen to me when I die?" (Solomon et al., 1998, p. 13).

In effect then, cultures give people a role to play, distracting them from the anxiety of worrying about what they fear most. Interestingly, this is often exactly what is recommended for socially anxious people — adopt a role. Cultures provide guidelines for immortality, either symbolically (for instance, amassing great fortunes that out-survive their originator) or spiritually (for instance, going to heaven). Abiding by cultural rules can thus provide an immortality of sorts, but perhaps even more important is its here-and-now function:

> The resulting perception that one is a *valuable* member of a *meaningful* universe constitutes *self-esteem*; and self-esteem is the primary psychological mechanism by which culture serves its death-denying function (Solomon et al., 1998, p. 13, italics in the original).

The U'wa's stance perhaps only seems so bizarre to us because we do not share with them a full appreciation of the life-serving (saving) and death-denying function of culture. Perhaps too often and for too long mental health professionals — especially psychologists — have stripped hapless mortals of their shaky beliefs and sent them out to discover their "true self". For example, Sheldon's Kopp's "If you see the Buddha on the road, shoot him", essentially tells us not to follow but to release oneself from the "oppression" of believing that someone else has the answer. Doubtless there is something in this stance but many may feel that to reduce ourselves *to only ourselves* is to deny many people the satisfaction, strength and meaning that they derive from feeling part of something greater than themselves (MacLachlan, 2003b).

However, it is easy to miss the subtly of TMT and to assume that it applies only to religious fanatics, "but not to me". It is therefore worth recounting just a couple of the experimental studies conducted to show how TMT may have relevance to us all, in some form, and how ultimately it is also of relevance to suicide. TMT is underpinned by two related, but distinct, hypotheses:

Self-esteem as an anxiety buffer

If self-esteem provides protection against anxiety, then strengthening self-esteem should reduce anxiety in response to subsequent threats.

The paradigm used to investigate this hypothesis is exemplified in an experiment by Solomon, Greenberg, Pyszczynski et al., (1991; Study One) where undergraduate student volunteers were told they were participating in a study examining the relationship between personality factors and emotionally arousing stimuli. All students completed personality questionnaires and were then provided with what they thought was highly personalised feedback regarding their responses. In fact, half of the group were all given the same feedback which was designed to *bolster their self esteem*. For example, their assessment stated: "While you may feel you have some personality weaknesses, your personality is fundamentally strong. Most of your aspirations tend to be pretty realistic." The other half were also all given the same feedback, but this was designed to be neutral with regard to their self-esteem: "While you have some personality weaknesses, you are generally able to compensate for them. Some of your aspirations may be a bit unrealistic." Students who received the positive feedback reported having higher self-esteem than those who received the neutral feedback (as measured by a subsequent assessment), showing that this temporary manipulation worked.

Next, each of the above groups were shown a seven-minute excerpt of a video called *Faces of Death* that included footage of an autopsy and an electrocution — clearly intended to be anxiety-provoking. Their self-reported anxiety was subsequently assessed and those who had received the positive personality feedback were found to be significantly less anxious as a results of seeing the video than those who received the neutral personality feedback. This supports the idea that temporarily enhancing self-esteem reduces anxiety in a death-related context. In a series of subsequent studies, it was demonstrated that the basic finding holds up for both trait (long term) and state (short term) high self-esteem, is independent of mood state, and generalise to other sort of threatening stimuli.

Culture as a mortality buffer[2]

If cultural world views provide protection against anxiety associated with thoughts of one's own death, then those who uphold similar values should be venerated, while those who violate them should be denigrated.

Again, we will only consider one of the experiments conducted to test this hypothesis in order to illustrate the paradigm used. Again, it is an imaginative and intriguing one. Their first study (Rosenblatt et al., 1989, Study One) was with volunteer municipal court judges from Tucson, Arizona. They were told that the researchers were interested in exploring the relationship between personality traits, attitudes and bond decisions (the sum of money that a defendant must pay prior to a trial in order to be released from prison). In addition, half the judges were given a mortality attitudes questionnaire (to make thoughts of mortality more salient) while the other half were not. The rest of the personality assessment was again a sham, except for a few questions given to the first group, which required open-ended responses, where they wrote out what they thought. These questions were: "Please briefly describe the emotions that the thought of your death arouses in you"; and "Jot down, as specifically as you can, what you think will happen to you as you physically die and once you are physically dead." All judges then completed several self-report checklists to assess the difference in their emotional reaction given that only half had been encouraged to think about death (there was no difference between the two groups of judges; one group was not more outwardly "upset" than the other).

All judges were then presented with a hypothetical case representative of those often submitted to judges before trial. The brief gave the arresting charge — prostitution — and the defendant's address, employment record, length of residence in the United States, and a copy of the arrest citation giving basic information such as arresting officer, place and time. Also, the prosecutor's opposition to releasing the defendant on their

---

[2] This is referred to as the "mortality salience hypothesis" throughout the many publications of Solomon, Greenberg, Pyszczynski and colleagues.

own recognisance, due to lack of community ties, was indicated in the brief. The judges had to set what they thought was the appropriate bond for the defendant. It is important to note here that the charge of prostitution was chosen because it is a crime that violates moral convictions espoused by North American culture. Also, judges are highly trained to make such decisions rationally and similarly across similar cases.

Those judges who wrote about their own death set an average bond of $455, while the judges who completed exactly the same procedures, except for writing about their own death, set an average bond of $50! The authors concluded that mortality salience increased the need for death-denying cultural world views and so provoked more extreme reactions to moral transgressors. Again, through many subsequent experiments, the general effect has been confirmed with other possible explanations ruled out. In fact, the findings seem to extend to defensive reactions, following mortality salience, towards others who are similar and dissimilar, in respect of both political and religious aspects of cultural worldview.

It would seem therefore that we are, through our socialisation, "locked into" a social system that needs others around us to agree with our view of the world. This is what culture is for. It is there to give us a life worth living, rather than to be exposed to a level of anxiety that is unbearable, and to continually contemplate our own ending. That is why we are so motivated to protect our worldviews. However, of crucial importance to us in our consideration of suicide is the finding that raising self-esteem eliminates the effects of mortality salience on our worldview. If a cultural worldview can bolter self-esteem and self-esteem is itself a product of a cultural construction of what is valued, how can esteem be accumulated to a sufficient degree, that it is no longer dependant on worldviews? This dilemma will be addressed in our final chapter.

When Cultures Change

"Cultural evolution" refers to the situation where values, attitudes and customs change within the same social system, over time (MacLachlan, 2003b). Use of the term here does not necessarily carry the connotations of biological evolution, where those "fittest" for the changing environment will prosper while those who do not "fit" will perish. Rather, we wish to emphasise the fact that the individual's adaptation to a changing cultural context (be it within or between cultures) is particularly demanding. The consequences of this will continue to be seen as cultures rush to change without considering the social and psychological consequences. The consequences of both the abandonment of traditional values and the eager adoption of "new" ideals need to be carefully considered.

Thus different historical epochs, although being characteristic of the same "national" culture, actually constitute very different social environments — cultures. Peltzer (1995, 2002) working in Africa, has described people living primarily traditional lives, those living primarily modern lives, and those who are caught between the two — "transitional people". Peltzer argues that socialisation is powerfully influenced by three dimensions — the authority dimension, the group dimension, and the body-mind-environment dimension. The transitional person, on their way to becoming a "modern" person, is no longer so influenced by traditional authority figures, is less under the influence of group norms. Furthermore, rites of passage seem empty rituals that fail to fulfil their reassuring and integrating roles; and technology and the emphasis on "the mind", diminish the importance of the cycles of nature and of physical contact between people. Clearly Peltzer's "transitional" people can be found throughout the world, including in its most "advanced" industrial societies, and those most rapidly "advancing" economically. What happens to people's values when their socio-economic context goes through rapid change?

Inglehart and Baker (2000) examined three waves of the World Values Survey (1981–82, 1990–91, and 1995–98), encompassing 65 societies on six continents, and apparently representative of three-quarters of the world population. They argue that the results provide strong evidence for both massive cultural change and the persistence of distinctive traditional values:

> A history of Protestant or Orthodox or Islamic or Confucian traditions gives rise to cultural zones with distinctive value

> systems that persist after controlling for the effects of economic development. Economic development tends to push societies in a common direction, but rather than converging, they seem to move on parallel trajectories shaped by their cultural heritages. We doubt that the forces of modernization will produce a homogenized world culture in the foreseeable future (p. 49, 2000).

In the Irish context, this would suggest that it is not simply a matter of "out with the old and in with the new", but of people finding a way to combine the old with the new. However, it is not that simple either.

Hermans and Kempen (1998) believe that the emphasis of conventional cross-cultural psychology on geographical location is becoming increasingly irrelevant. They instead emphasise the influence of interconnecting cultural and economic systems, of cultural hybridisation creating multiple identities, and of increasingly permeable cultural boundaries, all producing a multiplicity of meanings and practices and contributing to greater uncertainty. As Hermans and Kempen state, "uncertainty is not primarily in a culture's core but in its contact zones" (p. 1119, 1998). Thus a society need not now even go through particularly dramatic changes within its own "borders"; the extending arms of internationalisation and globalisation may grasp even those who are not active participants. In the case of the "Celtic Tiger", of course, these two forces interacted in a synergistic fashion, with internal change and powerful external political and economic forces quite literally "buying in" to these changes. In a sense, there are more margins to live on and perhaps the core is getting weaker. We should not be surprised therefore if the uncertainties of life are increasing. If the modern Ireland, with unprecedented immigration, increasing secularisation, economic prosperity and liberalisation of social attitudes (MacLachlan and O'Connell, 2000; O'Connell, 2001) can be distinguished from the Ireland of even just a decade ago (traditional, conservative, devout and often unemployed), then we could almost think of this transition as being similar to that which people experience when they move from one culture to another — usually across geographical boundaries.

"Celtic Tiger" Acculturation

Figure 3.1 illustrates what we think most people will agree is a dramatic relationship between male suicide and the rate of economic growth in Ireland over the past twenty years. While this relationship is clearly only correlational — it represents an *association* between suicide and economic growth rather than testifying to a causal relationship — its strength (for *males*; $r = .79$, $p < .001$ with GNP; $r = .75$, $p < .001$ with GDP and for *females*; $r = .59$, $p < .005$ with GDP and $r = .63$, $p < .005$) is nonetheless very impressive within the context of the social sciences (MacLachlan, 2003a). The fact that the relationship between the two economic indicators and female suicide is clearly weaker does imply a specific effect for males. In Chapter 5, and with specific reference to the male experience, we address the nature of the intervening variables between rate of economic growth and suicide. Here we are concerned to understand why there is any relationship at all between suicide and economic growth.

With regard to employment, in a mere two years (from 1998 to 2000) the numbers employed rose from 1,494,500 to 1,670,700, with the additional feature of an increase in population not solely due to births but as a result of immigration (O'Connell, 2001). As this was happening, the traditionally devout nation was seeing a change in the more spiritual side of things. While the Ireland of 1975 could certainly be seen as firmly committed to the Roman Catholic Church, recent figures show that this is no longer the case, with a steady decline in weekly Church attendance. O'Connell makes the significance of this change very clear. While a decline of about two per cent is seen each year, this has an overall significance such that by the year 2007 those attending mass every week would be in the minority — something not seen since the Famine. More than simple Church attendance, the number of people who state they believe in God has fallen, marking a change at both the behavioural and ideological levels (for further detail on this, and why it might be so, we recommend Chapter 5 of O'Connell, 2001).

Figure 3.1: Relationship between Economic Growth and Suicide Rate, 1981-2000

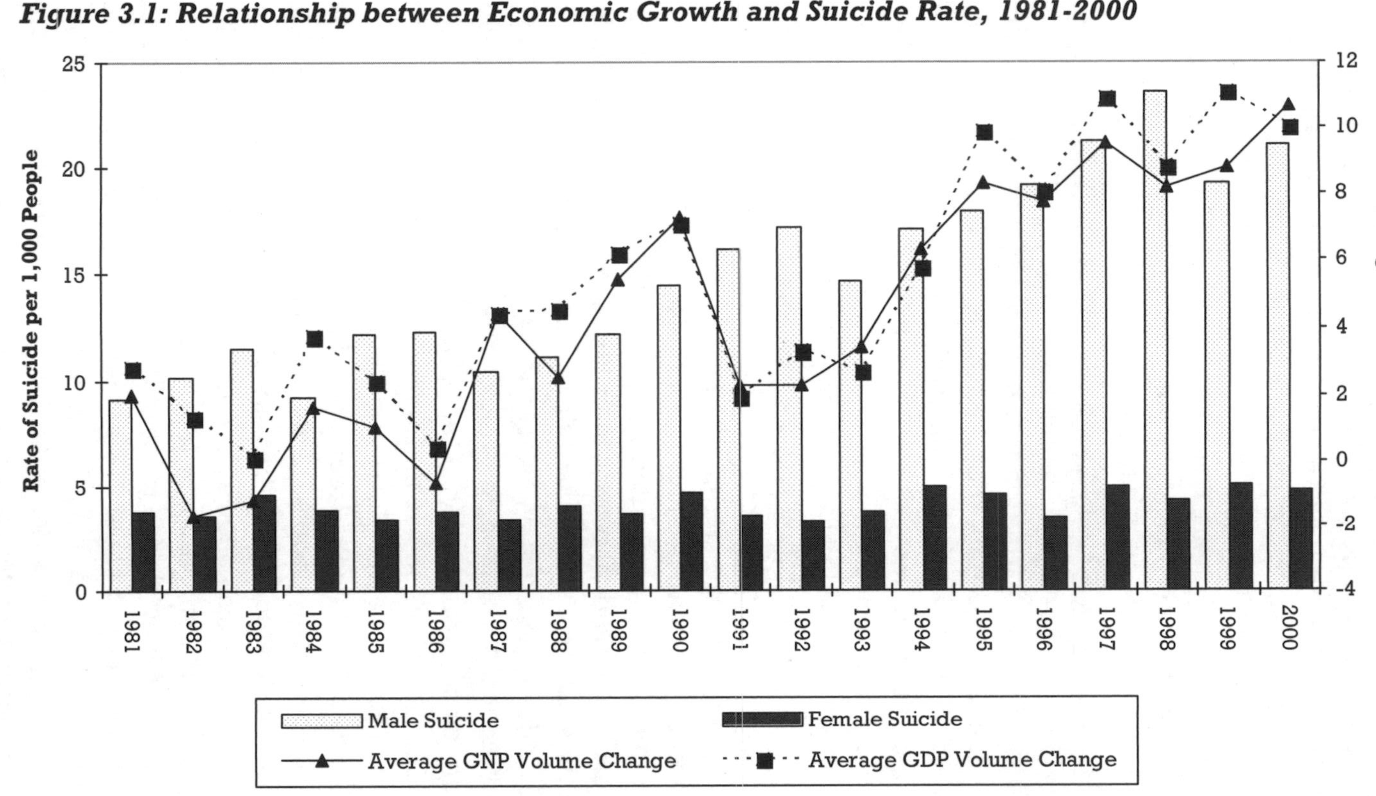

Thus the "Celtic Tiger" may be seen to be characterised by unprecedented levels of immigration, increasing secularisation, economic prosperity (that in years gone by could not even have been envisaged) and a general liberalisation of social attitudes — thus exhibiting what we term *temporal acculturation* (that is, culture change over time and within a nation). John Berry, the famous Canadian psychologist, developed a framework for understanding the effects of geographic acculturation (see Berry, 1997, for a review).

The people to whom this framework initially applied were refugees, immigrants and sojourners — people who had *geographically* moved from one culture to another. As a result of this cultural relocation, they had both home culture (the one into which they had been socialised) and host culture (the one to which they had moved) to deal with and psychologically integrate. It is important to note that elements at all levels — both individual and societal — are considered. More than simply saying that acculturation was the response of the individual to culture, *four* specific acculturation strategies were outlined. These strategies are *marginalisation* (where the individual fails to identify with either culture), *assimilation* (where the individual rejects their home culture and adopts the new), *separation* (where the individual retains their home culture despite the fact that they are now living in a different one, and fails to adopt the new culture) and finally, *integration* (where they successfully combine both cultures to which they have been exposed). When these were ordered in terms of their psychological healthiness, it was found that *integration* was the healthiest in terms of mental health (Berry and Kim, 1988).

MacLachlan, Smyth, Breen and Madden (submitted) investigated how Irish people have acculturated from traditional Ireland to "Celtic Tiger" Ireland. As an innovation to Berry's framework, we also allowed for an "uncertain" or "cultural ambivalence" classification, where participants gave mid-range responses to their desire to identify with the culture of "old Ireland" and "new Ireland". Eighty-eight per cent of over 700 respondents agreed that there had been a "big change in Irish culture over the past ten years" leading us to the conclusion that temporal acculturation was more than an abstract theoretical concept as it was salient to the majority of the sample. Importantly, however, it was those people who exhibited some degree of uncertainty or ambivalence who experienced poorest levels of mental health. While either being thoroughly caught up in Celtic Tiger Ireland or rejecting it in favour of a remembered traditional Ireland may not be the optimal situation in terms of psychological adjustment, well-being and functioning; but having *any* feeling towards the changes our own nation has recently experienced is relatively better than being uncertain, as it is this uncertainty, this lack of clarity and sensation of nebulousness, which appears to be problematic.

ANOMIE

In sociology, the implicit inclusion of culture has a long history originating with Durkheim's seminal work *Le Suicide* (1897/1951). In this work, generally seen as an interactive sociological theory (Kelleher, 1996), it was proposed that the element of *anomie* placed an individual at greater risk of suicide as the development of this characteristic indicated that the fundamental relationship between the individual and their society had been shattered.

Although some now argue that Durkheim's *Le Suicide* ought to be seen more as a demonstration of sociological methods than as a study of suicide, it remains one of the key texts discussing the social and cultural aspects of this issue. We rely heavily upon the various works of Steve Taylor, who has carried out detailed examinations of Durkheim's original text and the impact it has continued to have on the study of suicide.

At the time at which *Le Suicide* appeared, the nature of knowing about the world and the issues faced by people within the world was dominated by the positivist perspective — there were "truths" out there which could be both clearly observed and accurately collected. According to this approach, the same methodologies that had proved successful with the natural sciences could be applied to questions of humanity (such as suicide) with equally successful results and a "solution" could be reached.

Durkheim fundamentally disagreed and instead proposed that questions of humanity were essentially different, and instead argued in favour of a social science specific method of investigation. This idea remains to the present with sociology, psychology and other social sciences utilising specific qualitative and quantitative methods in their research.

At the time of publication (the first edition was published in 1897), there were two general schools of thought on suicide (Taylor, 1982). The first thought of suicide as a form of inherited madness while the second (which used comparative studies of official suicide rates) explained its occurrence in terms of various environmental factors. Both viewed suicide as an individual act and presented humankind as being quite uninvolved in their own fate — either madness or circumstance took over and determined the nature of their actions. On this point and with regard to future investigations of suicide, Morselli (1903) asserted that "The old philosophy of individualism had given to suicide the character of liberty and spontaneity, but now it became necessary to study it no longer as the expression of individual and independent faculties, but certainly as a social phenomenon allied with all the other racial [*sic*] forces" (*op cit*).

Indicative of the mood of the time, suicide numbers were collected alongside murder figures and rates of prostitution and alcoholism. In this way, suicide was deemed a question of morality rather than one to be tackled by science of any kind, including sociology and psychology.

It was into this era that Durkheim launched his new and altogether different perspective. No longer was suicide to be seen as the act of individual people but rather to be posed as a question for society more broadly. Society and culture were given primary importance in this alternative model. The degree of integration and regulation the individual experienced as a result of the type of society and culture in which they lived was seen to influence the likelihood of them contemplating the act of suicide. People were born into socio-cultural contexts which may be organised in a variety of ways but all of which hold a reality thoroughly independent of the individual. Thus, societal elements such as religious denomination and economic development were those of concern and each society was seen to have a certain capacity for suicide dependent on its structure at any given time (Durkheim, 1897/1951).

Specifically, Durkheim (1897/1951) delineated four types of suicide: egoistic, anomic, altruistic and the lesser-referred to mixed. Egoistic suicide resulted from a lack of integration of the individual into the society of which they are a part. Anomic suicide was presented as one which results from the state of modern economies. Here, the individual's needs and desires are determined by society and so, when any drastic change is experienced (such as a sudden increase in wealth) and the individual's horizons are broadened beyond what they can endure, suicide becomes more probable. Altruistic suicide, as it was conceived by Durkheim, is generally infrequent in contemporary Western society but continues to be seen in the form of suicide bombers and others who choose to end their lives for what they perceive as a "higher purpose". This type of suicide relates to the taking of one's own life for a "cause" such as political affiliation or religious sacrifice rather than reasons of personal circumstance and so was classed as an independent type.

Another important part of the argument was that suicide was seen as an entity *sui generis* and with more than one possible meaning, thus, albeit implicitly, the relativity of meaning had entered the arena. The issue of definition was not taken much beyond this point but, as we have already seen, it later became an issue of considerable debate and relevance as modern clinicians and researchers alike strive to determine the very nature of that which they study.

There was much to Durkheim's argument but, to illustrate, the religious aspect of his theory can be discussed in more detail. Judaism, Catholicism and Protestantism were each examined. With regard to those of the Jewish faith, the proposal was made that although their religion should generally protect against suicide, this was not reflected in the statistics but was explained in terms of a disproportionate number of Jewish individuals living in urban settings — a risk factor for suicide independent of the religion in question.

On the issue of Catholic versus Protestant suicide, the general proposal was that Catholics were less likely than Protestants to carry out a suicidal act given the level of integration their religion provided and despite the fact that both religions equally condemn suicide (in Ireland this could be seen as less accurate given the extensive social sanctions on issues of burial etc. for those who take their own lives). Protestants, in essence, traditionally stand alone with God and were permitted a far greater level of individual inquiry. Catholics, in contrast, were required by official Church policy not to read the bible themselves but to engage in religious worship as a congregation and with the leadership of an appropriately ordained priest. Catholics at this time were not permitted to investigate their own religion, either in historical or present form, but expected to accept it in totality and relinquish control of conscience to the "divine" power of the Lord. The one situation in which this "trend" is reversed is where those of the Protestant faith are in the minority in which case the religious risk factor (as conceived by Durkheim) decreases.

It is hard to believe in the protective nature of the Catholic faith, given the increase in suicide in Ireland, one of the most traditionally Catholic countries. More important than the specifics of the theory, however, is the way in which questions were posed, the opening of inquiry beyond what had previously been known and the inclusion of culture and society at a time this was unheard of.

The point of recounting these ideas is to illustrate the various and complex ways in which culture has been considered to be related to suicide. It is no less likely that Ireland has sociocultural structures that are supportive of suicide — it may simply be the case that they have not been sought, or if found have not been recognised as such.

Just as old Ireland attempted to drive out the demons of suicide by driving a stake through the heart of its victims, modern Ireland attempts to simply drive *past* uncomfortable, stigmatised issues such as suicide. With such a blinkered perspective, it is very much the case that the cultural perspective has not been tried and found wanting, but rather that it has been found wanting and somewhat inconvenient and so not tried.

It always seems easier and more straightforward to examine *other* cultures in a rational and wholly dispassionate way, not least because they are that — other. This is not necessarily premeditated but is more generally a feature of human psychology (Freud built an entire theory on the basis of our inability to be completely rational and unbiased). There is always the temptation to protect and value what is your own, even if you know it to be less than perfect. Alongside this, there exists the fear that if you begin to look, or alternatively allow others to look, something will be found amiss, the tarnish will appear. But this does not have to be the case. By proposing a cultural analysis, we are not suggesting that traditional Irish heritage be devalued; rather, we wish to acknowledge that "change" and "progress" are not synonymous and suggest instead a mature and reflective examination of those negative aspects of our culture that have developed over time.

Chapter 4

WHY YOUTH?

Youth, which is forgiven everything, forgives itself nothing: age, which forgives itself everything, is forgiven nothing — George Bernard Shaw

The young always have the same problem — how to rebel and conform at the same time. They have now solved this by defying their parents and copying each other. — Quentin Crisp

We begin this chapter as we left off the last one. We start by considering the very idea of adolescence, critically reviewing the "storm and stress" image, and then move to specifically address the issues of childhood suicide and adolescent suicide. We then examine "youth culture" and specific "sub-cultural" aspects of it that have been suggested to be associated with suicide. We end the chapter by looking at the idea of cultural continuity as suicide prevention.

A NEWLY CREATED LIFE-STAGE

Adolescence is challenging for the adult world because it questions adult values. It is a time when boundaries are pushed and the very existence of *self* is investigated and experimented with.

There was a time in Western culture, however, when "adolescence" simply did not exist. Individuals were expected to move from being a child to being an adult with no stage of transition. In this way, recent authors make the point that adolescence is something of a modern creation; more specifically, that it is the "luxury" and "invention" of affluent, predominantly Western, democratic nations (Curran, 1987). When resources were scarce and humankind had to contend daily with issues of survival in the most basic sense, there was no time or place for adolescents to "discover themselves". The individual was either a child (who had to be cared for and was not capable of supporting themselves) or they were a productive, vital member of society (an adult). Robertson (1990) makes the further point that it is only since the need for an educated workforce of ever-increasing professionalism emerged that this "life-stage" has been constructed in its full glory.

While the emergence of adolescence has offered the psychological time and space for an individual to fully consider the questions of what and who they will be when they "grow up", it also offers almost limitless choice (although this does not hold for all socioeconomic groups). Curran (1987) argues that this is both positive and negative — positive in the sense that young adults are no longer simply "put to work" and are given the opportunity to choose their own life path, but negative in that the adolescents of today are also free to fail.

A further factor to consider is that adolescence is essentially being lengthened: tasks which in the past were symbolic of adulthood — such as getting one's first job, moving out of the parental home, making a home for oneself, marriage and having children — are now taking place at a later stage (if at all). While on one hand this may be taken as a sign of "progress", it also presents issues that will have to be dealt with in developmental terms if psychological health is to be maintained. What we currently have is perhaps something of a dangerous mix — a society that has created adolescence, but which also places extreme pressure (for success, development and material attainment) on its young people. Adolescents are now *required* to find identity and become involved in a society that is quite capable of marginalising, alienating and confusing them. There is therefore a danger of people receiving a mixed message: that *all* are capable of great depths of self-knowledge and happiness, but fail in this and you have failed not only the societal task but oneself also. Increasingly, there is a "psychologising" of our culture, taking after the North American fixation with the notion that "everybody has some potential" and they *ought* to maximise it.

Kenny (2001) examines this concept in greater depth with her work prefaced by the assertion that ours is a postmodern society which holds implications for all areas of existence, including adolescent mental health. She makes the point that we live in a world with fewer certainties than ever before and individuals — perhaps especially youth — are faced with issues that previous generations simply did not have to consider. When the impact of a postmodern world is considered with regard to the development of self and identity, Giddens (1991) asserts that much of this developmental task depends on the evolution and establishment of trust. It is this essential leap of faith that is required if secure social interactions are to be experienced. Kenny's proposal is that the postmodern situation of uncertainty and multiple choice in almost every area of life does not facilitate (and may even hinder) this development of trust, and so relates to issues of identity confusion and may even extend to the development of depression and suicidal behaviour. Specifically, the Irish cultural milieu in which we find ourselves in this early part of the twenty-first century is replete with images of *distrust* — the clergy abuse, doctors kill, corrupt politicians steal and cheat.

Who we are (the very core "self" of being) has come to be determined by what we can buy and own, the materialism and consumerism of which O'Connell (2001) speaks. The overwhelming message being broadcast is that you are only as good as what you can buy, as our traditional cultural icons are being eroded and replaced by McDonalds, Nike, BMW and the like. The *No Logo* world which Naomi Klein (2000) outlined has without doubt hit our shores and taken firm root. The constant bombardment of our culture with "Americanised" images and values can be seen daily, while at the same time traditional cultural icons and role models are now ridiculed, feared and reviled. If we were left in any doubt about the impact of such uncertainty and distrust on our young people, the suicide figures for Ireland since 1990 clearly indicate that something maladaptive and "unhealthy" is taking place.

Adolescence as Pathology?

Some authors, such as Haim (1974), have suggested that adults cannot hope to understand the experience of the adolescent, such are the extreme and contradictory emotions involved. Haim also refers to alienation and any number of misconceptions that may occur between adolescents and adults that may obscure the accurate assessment of adolescent behaviour. Some therefore argue that this leads to insurmountable obstacles in effective communication between adults and adolescents. Apart from this perspective holding little popular appeal, it is also an unduly pessimistic view of adolescence as a life-stage and the potential co-operation that may take place between generations. Haim, however, is not alone in this gloomy outlook.

The idea that adolescence is a time of inescapable "storm and stress", characterised by moodiness, the tendency to contradict one's parents and the emergence of risky behaviour (Arnett, 1999), among other things, originated from the psychology of G. Stanley Hall's writing in 1904 (as cited in Arnett, ibid) where it was claimed that the teenage years are inevitably filled with "*sturm und drang*" (storm and stress). While Hall allowed for individual differences and socio-cultural effects (in the proposition that modern Western lifestyles, replete with increasing urbanisation, lead to a conflict between teenagers' need for adventure and society's promotion of a sedentary lifestyle), the idea that a "teenage storm" was inescapable was firmly held by psychologists for a long time. Among them was Anna Freud (1958, 1968, 1969), who proposed that those adolescents who *did not* experience "storm and stress" were, in fact, exhibiting some form of psychopathology. In this way, adolescence as a developmental stage was, for a time at least, pathologised: if difficulty and disturbance were *not* experienced, pathology was present; and if disturbances *were* experienced, then obviously (according to this line of thinking) pathology was present!

Such a ridiculous pathologising of this developmental period could result in real states of distress being overlooked, or alternatively, could normalise deviant or destructive behaviours. Arnett (1999) presents a more acceptable alternative, such that adolescence may be seen as a time when certain difficulties are more likely, but that this is by no means inevitable. Instead, adolescence is to be seen as a challenging, sometimes difficult period, which can be successfully mastered by most. Many adolescents will never think about suicide, and the vast majority of those who *do* (either in an objective, philosophical manner or with regard to their own existence) will never make an attempt of any form. Furthermore, of the small number who may behave in a suicidal manner, most will never complete a suicide. However, some will and it is this smaller group with whom we are concerned.

In closing this section, we return to Kenny (2001) who asserts that rather than place emphasis on the pathological in an attempt to understand child and adolescent suicide, focus should be placed on the *phenomenological*. Is it the case that adolescence, generally, is a time of reduced tolerance for a feeling of being unable to cope? Is it that adolescents (who often feel invincible) are more vulnerable to perceived failures at this time, as it so directly contrasts with their vision of themselves? Or, is it that they are less likely to ask for help and support given that one of the main "tasks" at this stage of development is the attainment of autonomy? It is unlikely that any single piece of work (our own included) will be able to answer all of these questions. The importance of this focus, though, cannot be underestimated, not only because it allows for a consideration of those socio-cultural factors to which we have referred throughout, but it also takes the important step towards making suicide available for discussion, outside of psychiatric, criminal or taboo settings. This is *not* to promote suicide, but removes the distancing and distracting character with which suicide has long been imbued.

CHILDHOOD SUICIDE

Much of our resistance to the very concept of child suicide stems from our reluctance to view childhood as anything other than happy and carefree. If a child is capable of actively making a decision to end their own life, then they present a picture that is one of depression, hopelessness and deep unhappiness. But this is not the picture we have of childhood or children, nor is it one we ever want to have. Although, thankfully, childhood suicide is relatively rare (both internationally and in the Republic of Ireland) this too has seen a limited increase. In the Republic since 1990 there have been a total of 41 deaths by suicide in the five- to fourteen-year-old age group. While our consideration here is of adolescent suicide predominantly, it is always important to bear in mind that adolescent individuals emerge not from a vacuum, devoid of any psychological experience, but from a childhood with its rich, complex and sometimes despairing mixture of life experiences. Therefore, a brief examination of suicide in childhood is warranted.

Dominian (1990) cites the work of Lourie (1957) as the first and most thorough examination of youth suicide. Some of the earliest reports of suicide in young children emerged from late eighteenth-century Prussia. If we return for a moment to the definition of suicide we selected from Shneidman (1985, p. 203) — that "currently in the Western world, suicide is a conscious act of self-induced annihilation, best understood as a multidimensional malaise in a needful individual who defines an issue for which the suicide [*sic*] is perceived as the best solution" — we see that many issues surrounding an act being deemed suicidal rests with the individual's conscious knowledge and understanding of the implications and consequences of their behaviour. The question therefore becomes whether or not children are capable of intending, planning and executing such behaviours.

Kenny (2001) cites the work of Aries (1960) who summarises what was known as *preformation theory*. In short, this theory holds that children are miniature adults from the time of implantation in the uterus. According to this theory, the child is a fully formed person who, like an adult, is fully aware of the consequences of their behaviour, and consequently is to be held responsible for them. If one were to subscribe to this view, children would clearly be capable of *meaning* to kill themselves (thus, capable of suicide). Western societies, however, do not generally accept this view and instead see children as qualitatively different from adults. They are born dependent and in need of dutiful care. They are accorded special rights and privileges by society and are generally deemed "immature" until adulthood is reached (note that the definition of "adulthood" is also open to cultural interpretation). Interesting, though, Kenny argues that this perspective does not automatically mean that children are unable to knowingly take their own lives. Such a conclusion needs to be carefully considered.

One of the key developmental tasks of childhood is the ability to successfully differentiate alternative states of existence, among them death (Anthony, 1971). There is much to suggest that a child's understanding of death is different to that of an adult and that it does not develop in a random disorganised manner, but in line with the stages of general cognitive development (Piaget, 1965). In order to reach what is termed a *mature conceptualisation of death*, elements of *non-functionality* (when you are dead you cannot behave as you do when alive), *irreversibility* (death is permanent and cannot be undone) and *universality* (a recognition of the mortality of all of humanity, themselves included) need to be firmly established (Cuddy-Casey and Orvaschel, 1997).

The aforementioned Piagetian theory of cognitive development proposes that the various stages of development are acquired as a function of age, with an understanding of death considered to fall under the stage of concrete operational thinking (occurring between seven and twelve years). This is the stage where *conservation of quantity* (e.g. despite the different appearance of liquid in a short, stout glass, and liquid in a tall thin glass, the same quantity is involved), *classification of objects* (into plants, animals, etc.), ability to understand *rule-governed games*, adoption of *geographic perspective* for another (e.g. my right, as I look at you face-to-face, is your left), simple *manipulation of numbers* (addition, subtraction, multiplication and division), and the introduction of *use of logic* are attained.

Kane (1979) applied this framework to the development of the concept of death and found that a stage-model was appropriate. In the first stage (corresponding to Piaget's preoperational stage, two to five years approximately) children adopted an egocentric, almost magical perspective and assumed that death was a form of separation (thus not irreversible). At the second stage (which broadly corresponds to Piaget's concrete operational stage, approximately five to twelve years), the child had moved to a point where death was seen as concrete and externally caused, which corresponds to other cognitive development seen at this stage (outlined above). In time, and still during this second stage, internal causation of death came to be understood, but the mature conceptualisation still had not been reached. Finally, in the third stage (corresponding to Piaget's formal operational stage which extends into adulthood) children were seen to develop the ability to think about death in abstract terms and consider hypothetical alternatives surrounding the issue.

However, other writers, such as Speece and Brent (1992), have proposed that children reach a reasonably mature understanding at an earlier age — between five and seven years — and so this issue remains unresolved. As with all developmental theories, however, they should not be taken as an absolute "blueprint" to which all children adhere, but rather as providing some general information on the age at which most children come to understand death in terms that correspond to adult thinking. In addition, Speece et al. assert that the achievement of the concept of irreversibility may not be a case of "all or nothing", but rather progress over time, thus allowing for individual difference (including the important feature of exposure to, or experience with, death).

One of the foremost writers in *thanatology* (that is, the formal study of death and death-related phenomena), Robert Kastenbaum, makes the point that while cognitive theories such as those briefly outlined above are certainly useful, it is essential to remember that even the youngest child is capable of experiencing separation and the resultant feelings of loss, anxiety and sadness. If death is seen as the ultimate form of separation, irrespective of language development (which may preclude the child from verbalisation of feelings), some form of understanding of death is held from the earliest experiences of the child's separation from their primary caregiver, albeit formally classified as an immature conceptualisation (Kastenbaum, 2001). Kenny (2001) makes the point that immature conceptualisations may represent death as a form of being in another dimension, where the dead can look upon the living in an almost sleep-like state (and where return to the living world is possible). The troubling aspect of this conceptualisation is that, if so believed, some children may seek death as a temporary release from a stressful, distressing or unhappy situation. So as to whether or not children are capable of suicide, the answer appears to be a qualified "yes"; however the motivation and meaning of the act differs from adolescent and adult suicides.

Numerous studies have shown that the child's view of death may, in certain situations, serve to facilitate suicidal behaviour. Orbach and Glaubman (1978) found that suicidal children held a more complex and possibly erroneous perception of their own death than non-suicidal children. These suicidal children attributed living qualities to the state of death. They believed in the continuation of life after death and in the possible return to life from a state of death. These beliefs were held by suicidal children more often than matched control groups of violent and non-suicidal groups. In another study, Orbach and Glaubman (1978) argued that suicidal individuals are threatened by their suicidal thinking and that, in order to overcome this threat, they distort their death concept to one which sees death as pleasurable and reversible. Pfeffer et al. (1979, 1980, 1984) in a series of studies working with suicidal children who were inpatients, non-suicidal inpatient children and "normal" school children found that suicidal children (across all groups) believed that death is a temporary, pleasant state which will relieve all tensions. Furthermore, Pfeffer (1986) has asserted that suicidal children show fluctuations in their death concepts such that in times of stress, or during a crisis, a regression is seen to an earlier understanding of death.

Considering these factors, Stillion and McDowell (1996) offer a model for suicidal behaviour generally (the *Suicide Trajectory Model*), which provides sufficient flexibility to be applied to various age groups (model presented in Table 4.1). While this framework offers a good summary of many salient issues from suicide research and literature, it is completely devoid of any cultural insight — an issue to which we will later return.

In such a brief review of child suicide as ours, it is impossible to present detailed information on each of these elements and we refer the interested reader to Stillion and McDowell (1996) for additional information.

Table 4.1: The Suicide Trajectory Model Applied to Child Suicide

Age	Biological Risk Factors	Psychological Risk Factors	Cognitive Risk Factors	Environmental Risk Factors	Warning Signs	Triggering Events
5-14	Impulsivity	Feelings of inferiority	Immature views of death	Early loss	Truancy	Minor life events
		Expendable child syndrome	Concrete operational thinking	Parent conflict	Poor school performance	
			Attraction to and repulsion from life and death	Inflexible family structure	Anxiety	
				Unclear family member roles	Sleep disturbance	
				Abuse and neglect	Aggression	
				Parent suicidal behaviour	Impulsiveness	
					Low frustration tolerance	

Source: Stillion et al., 1997

Adolescent Suicide

Despite the fact that many studies of adolescent suicide are based on clinical samples, recent authors suggest that the majority of adolescents who engage in some form of suicidal behaviour will never enter into a clinical setting because of it, thus calling the assertions of more traditional approaches into question (De Wilde, 2000). Despite this, the predominant focus of much of this work has been on the biomedical approach to understanding suicidal behaviour. According to O'Connor and Sheehy (2000), in its purist form, this approach does not recognise a link between mind and body (that is, each is said to act independently of the other); health and illness are seen as discrete experiences (rather than existing on a continuum where one can experience some form of ill-health but class oneself more generally as "healthy"); and, although proponents recognise that illness can have a psychological impact, the reverse relationship is not accepted: that psychological factors themselves can cause ill-health.

When this approach is applied to the investigation of suicide, what results is a reductionist picture which sees suicide as the eventual outcome of mental illness, neuropsychological defect or general medical conditions. No *meaningful* reference is made to any of the social or cultural factors to which we seek to draw attention. Despite this, the biomedical approach has many followers who are attracted to its apparent certainty and rigour, feeling that to look at socio-cultural factors is not only beyond the scope of what can reasonably be determined as a "valid" area of inquiry but that the inclusion of such elements, in opposition to the reductionist biomedical perspective, is generally irrelevant.

In this section on adolescent suicide, we present information on the alternative ways in which suicide has been understood socially and culturally.

Early Experiences and Subsequent Suicidal Behaviour

Various risk factors may lead adolescents to the point of suicide. Some of these include family discord, lack of support and general familial dysfunction (Dubow, Kausch, Blum, Reed and Bush, 1989; Garrison, Addy, Kirby, McKeown, and Waller,

1991). This unsettled type of familial milieu has long been linked to the experience of major depression but also holds clear links to the subsequent development of suicidal behaviours (Reinherz et al., 1993). Another element to be considered is the feeling of not being valued as a family member and the experience of aggression or violence from other family members or within the family setting. This latter element, however, has been linked to the development of suicidal ideation in females only, suggesting different distal and proximal risk factors for males (Reinherz et al., 1995). Health problems, specifically those of a chronic nature (Blumenthal and Kupfer, 1988, Lewinsohn, Rohde, and Seeley, 1993); the experience of negative or traumatic life events (Garrison et al., 1991); and academic problems (Lewinsohn et al., 1993) have also been presented as risk factors for the emergence of suicidal behaviour.

While this body of literature is clearly useful in the examination of some of the possible causes of suicide, a clear pathway to suicide remains to be determined. Reinherz et al. (1995) took up this challenge by following a group of 400 Boston children from age five to eighteen and examining those early psychosocial elements (that is, occurrences at age five) which were seen to lead to increased risk of suicidal behaviour by mid-adolescence (age fifteen).

When early risk factors for *males* were examined, it was seen that a clear pattern of behavioural, emotional and interpersonal problems was successfully capable of differentiating between suicidal and non-suicidal groups. This pattern was identifiable by both mothers and teachers from the age of five right through to mid-adolescence (age fifteen). At age five, those who would later develop suicidal ideation were rated by their mothers as significantly more dependent than non-suicidal counterparts. By age nine, both mothers and teachers were able to outline a constellation of behaviours such that the suicidal group were recognised as experiencing higher levels of anxiety and poorer socio-emotional adjustment overall. Interestingly, while others were able to observe clear differences in those who would go on to become suicidal (versus those who would not) the boys themselves showed no differences in their self-perception, perceived unpopularity and levels of anxiety or unhappiness. Thus, the degree to which the children were self-aware of the difficulties they were evidently experiencing was low.

Those who would go on to become ideators were also more than twice as likely to have developed a psychological disorder by age fourteen and were more than four times more likely (than non-ideator counterparts) to have developed two or more disorders by this age, along with the aforementioned emotional and behavioural difficulties. Specific early-onset disorders experienced included simple phobia, alcohol abuse and drug abuse/dependence.

For *females*, a slightly different pattern was seen. Early behavioural and emotional problems and poor self-perception (that is, seeing oneself as worthless, having low self-esteem etc.) increased risk of the development of suicidal behaviours by mid-adolescence in females. Female ideators were more than twice as likely to hold poorer perceptions of their role in the family (seen from age nine) and were more than three times more likely to report serious family arguments, which included the occurrence of violence (between the ages of ten and fourteen) than non-suicidal counterparts. While in early childhood both mothers and teachers rated the girls who would go on to be suicidal as being more aggressive, shy and dependent; this pattern was no longer observable by age nine. Thus, the outward constellation of behaviours seen in boys over all eleven years (ages five to fifteen inclusive) was not seen across this same duration in girls. Furthermore, unlike the at-risk boys who did not rate themselves any differently than the non-suicidal group, the at-risk girls thought themselves to be more anxious, unhappy and unpopular than counterparts (perceptions which, in and of themselves, may have led to the development of depression and/or hopelessness).

Although Reinherz et al. (1995) made brief reference to the significant role played by traumatic or stressful life events, it is the work of Beautrais et al. (1997) which more clearly outlines this link. These authors examined those events which precipitated a serious suicide attempt ("serious" was defined in terms of the individual requiring hospitalisation above and beyond the normal period of observation following an act of self-harm, and those cases which required more intense medical intervention, such as hospitalisation in a specialised unit such as Intensive Care). Precipitating events are seen to generally fall under four broad themes: interpersonal conflict, economic problems, school-related difficulties and legal or disciplinary problems (Brent and Moritz, 1993; De Wilde, 2000). The frequency with which these various precipitating experiences are reported differs, to the extent that Hawton et al. (1982) found a sizeable proportion of their sample unable to clearly articulate or attribute any reason for their parasuicidal act. One possible explanation for this may be that this area is replete with methodological difficulties in obtaining motivational information: there may be a time delay between the suicidal behaviour and questioning regarding motivation may have memory effects; mental state (such as the experience of depression and hopelessness) may affect the likelihood of certain events being reported; and the fact that the suicidal behaviour has taken place at all may lead to a degree of "effort after meaning" in order to explain the behaviour to others.

Beautrais et al. (1997) attempted to overcome these difficulties by obtaining motivational reports not only from the adolescents themselves but also from a nominated "significant other" who was sufficiently familiar with their general state and life circumstances to be able to offer a reliable account of those experiences that occurred in the twelve months preceding the suicidal behaviour. Most commonly, these serious suicide attempts were precipitated by relationship breakdowns or other interpersonal problems. (Note that although this is in direct contrast to Boergers et al.'s (1998) research, mentioned below, there is a substantial difference in the samples included in the research, such that those included here, where interpersonal issues *were* a feature, were also those exclusively classified as "serious", and so some variation is to be expected.) Difficulties with family, financial difficulties, legal problems and difficulties in school were also commonly reported. The reports given by the individuals themselves and their significant other were remarkably similar, which leads to the conclusion that although the suicide attempt is itself a traumatic life event, people are capable of accurate recollection of those circumstances which led to the point of suicide.

Thus, from these findings it can be said that although different in quality for boys and girls, and inherently complex in nature, a clear phenomenological sequence can be traced from childhood to adolescence which leads the individual to the point of suicidal ideation and/or behaviour.

If these are some of the experiences that lead young people to the point of suicidal behaviour in adolescence, it is also important to examine the "whys" of suicide, as told by the individuals themselves. That is, a detailed consideration of the motivations which adolescents ascribe to their own suicidal behaviours is called for. This type of investigation also holds importance if education and prevention programmes are to succeed, as a good "match" between adolescent needs and programme provision is vital if any success is to be achieved.

Contrary to long-held beliefs, contemporary understanding of the principal motivation for suicidal behaviour is *not* the communication of distress (as in a "cry for help" that is so often referred to); nor is it an attention-seeking behaviour. The vast majority of adolescents who attempt to take their own lives report that their primary motivation is a wish to die, closely followed by the desire to escape and the need to obtain relief (Shneidman, 1990; Stone, 1999). Rarely were more manipulative motivations, such as making people sorry, endorsed (Hawton et al., 1982). Williams (1986) also links these findings to the level of hopelessness experienced by the individual, such that the higher the level of hopelessness, the greater is the explicit wish to die.

In a detailed study in this vein, Boergers et al. (1998) took a multifaceted approach, examining factors across emotional, behavioural and familial spheres. Prior to commencement of the study, these authors thought that those adolescents who reported their motivation as an explicit wish to die would also be seen to experience higher levels of hopelessness, anger, depression, loneliness and socially prescribed perfectionism and poorer family functioning than adolescents who reported alternative motivations. These expectations were supported.

Suicide clearly cannot therefore ever be reduced to the level of a desperate act of communication, an attempt to evoke a reaction, obtain sympathy or achieve manipulative ends. For the majority of those who progress as far as actively and intentionally carrying out a suicidal behaviour, the objective is clear — they no longer want to be alive.

The most commonly endorsed motivations (as they currently appear in the literature) for suicidal behaviours are *intra*personal rather than *inter*personal. Thus, the source of these behaviours is described in terms of the individual's own psychological state rather than as a result of their relationships with others. While this an important piece of information for those left behind by the suicide of a loved one, and points to the extreme and often unobservable internal state of distress of those who take their own lives, it also gives us some further insight into the weakness of current approaches and their failure to link the intra- and interpersonal. To bring the individual and their context together is something that has yet to be done.

To reach a point where one considers taking one's own life is a tragic conclusion in itself, even if not acted upon. In order to understand the fundamental role played by intrapersonal issues in youth suicide, we propose that the sort of relationship one has with oneself is a *product* of how one *reads* (thus understands and gives meaning to) one's place in the social and cultural world — that is, the individual's own *cultural drama* and *narrative history*. Thus, both interpersonal and socio-cultural elements are vital in determining the tone and nature of one's intrapersonal experiences; thus making the link between the person and their culture in suicidal behaviour more salient.

Youth Culture

Youth culture is defined by Rice (1996) as "the sum of ways of living of adolescents; it refers to the body of norms, values and practices recognized and shared by members of the adolescent society as appropriate guides to actions". Amit-Talai (1995) makes the point that it is never to be seen as an isolated factor, as it is always part of a larger cultural setting in which individuals find themselves. Nonetheless, elements specific to youth culture warrant consideration, as these differentiate "youth" from society at large. Janssen et al. (1999) assert that youth culture itself can play a protective role, acting as a source of self-esteem and playing a critical part in the development of self-identity.

While the combination of youth and death appears paradoxical at first, death may be particularly salient to today's youth. Janssen et al. (1999) argue that during one of the key tasks of adolescence — the emergence of a coherent concept of self — the teenager is forced (often by society) to examine their future and their role in the world. In a society which places extreme emphasis on career-based roles, death is even more salient to the point that in certain cultures (specifically, in Janssen et al., the Netherlands) a youth culture that focuses on death instead of life has come to exist. Curran (1987) also draws attention to this contradictory link between youth and death, referring to youth suicide as that "monstrous coupling of two incompatible facts, youth and death, which throw our sense of meaning and order into chaos". Thus, the possible link between youth suicide and culture has been tentatively established.

Rock 'n' Roll and Youth Suicide: Specific Elements of Youth Culture

Seca (1991) has stressed the positive effects of youth culture in the emergence of one's own identity and lifestyle. Arnett (1991) proposes that specific elements, such as rock music, have a protective function, acting as a form of coping mechanism or medium for vicarious release. Looking at the relationship between musical preference and suicide is interesting because it draws on sociological elements of suicidology and, as such, illustrates a further link between cultural elements and the issue of youth suicide.

Rock music and the identification with this subculture is perhaps one of the most researched questions in this area. For many years, there has existed a concern over the relationship between heavy metal music (HM) and youth suicide. Parents, teachers and healthcare professionals in contact with adolescents have expressed concern over the effect of explicit references in songs to sex, drugs, Satanism, deviance and suicidal behaviour. Heavy metal is said to have been born of the demise of the "Peace, Love and Happiness" mood of the 1960s, offering instead pessimism and a grey-toned lens through which to cynically view the world (Stack, Gundkach and Reeves, 1994). These authors also argue that the metal subculture is characterised by two primary forms of chaos: personal and social. The former relates to feelings of depression, social isolation and failed personal relationships where no possibility of solution to these problems is seen. It is primarily this aspect which is seen to relate to mental health.

While Stack et al. (1994) concluded that HM fans share many risk factors with those classed as moderate to high risk of suicide, they also assert that HM music may foster already-present suicidal tendencies in this group, rather than create them. Others, such as Lester and Whipple (1996), have argued that although there may be a relationship between *past* suicidal ideation and HM fanship, no *current* relationship was observed in their own research. Raviv et al. (1996) offered an alternative interpretation, based on Israeli research. In this case, it was argued that adolescents' preoccupation with HM and their wish to identify with this highly recognisable subculture may be seen as an attempt to seek separation from their parents and find some degree of autonomy in the world. In this way, music preference was seen to be directly related to identity emergence and could, for the most part, be seen more as a positive than negative element of youth development.

Stack (1998) took the investigation a step further, examining the link between attitudes towards suicide and adolescent music preference. This complements nicely the other work that has been done by authors such as King et al. (1996) on attitudes towards suicide in youth populations. In short, those who are classed as "metalers" are non-religious, which is, independently, a risk for suicidal behaviours. Further, when the lyrics of some of the more popular songs are examined, clear references to suicide are seen, with Ozzy Osbourne's "Suicide Solution" being one cited example. While the artist may not have intended a link to suicide — indeed Weinstein (1991) makes the point that the song actually tackled the issue of alcohol abuse — Bryson (1996) argues that the fan base must be remembered. He proposes that many of the hardcore fans are not highly educated and may, in fact, interpret the lyrics, thus adding to their suicidal risk. What is perhaps more important from a psychological perspective is the sense of hopelessness that is so tangible in this subculture. Problems are identified either at a personal or societal level, but no solution or successful role model is presented. Instead, these difficulties are portrayed as insurmountable, with death, for some, being seen as the only "out". Such was the conclusion reached by Gaines (1991), who spent a year living with HM fans in New Jersey, North America. She reported that one of the clearest and certainly most visible signs of this hopelessness was the wrist scars from former suicidal behaviour on so many of the teenagers.

Copycat Suicide and Media Coverage

One of the most famous cases of a rock-related celebrity suicide is that of Nirvana star, Kurt Cobain. Jobes et al. (1996) examined in detail the possible effect that such a visible and media-driven suicide had on the vulnerable population of the Seattle area (the location of Cobain's death) and whether or not the *Werther effect*, relating to imitative or copycat suicides (Phillips, 1974) was observed in its aftermath. The authors summarise Cobain's oft-troubled and complicated life: he had received a diagnosis of hyperactivity at the age of eight and this marked the beginning of a problematic existence. In *Rolling Stone* magazine some four months prior to his death, he openly talked about his chronic suicidal ideation and preoccupation with guns. His body was found on 8 April 1994 by a workman. He had died from a gunshot wound to the head, with additional toxicological analysis showing high levels of heroin and Valium. He was 27 years old and was recognised at the time as being a cultural icon for an entire generation. In response to news of his death, MTV ran a Nirvana special with 24-hour showing of the band's music videos. The Seattle Crisis Clinic (which dealt with mental health crisis intervention for the surrounding area) reported immediate media interest with questions being posed as to the nature of suicide and the risk Nirvana fans were at. In response, the Clinic listed the warning signs that precipitate a suicidal act and its number was presented in all media coverage of the event. The authors report that in the seven weeks following Cobain's death, there were in fact fewer suicides than for the same period the previous year.

The one case cited as being copycat in nature was that of a 28-year-old man who, after attending a candlelight vigil in memory of Cobain, returned home and ended his life, also with a shotgun. He was known to have every Nirvana album, be a heavy substance abuser with a history of suicidal ideation and a father who had died by the same method. Thus, while his death may have superficially appeared to be the result of an imitative act, many contextual factors and the individual's own history appear more directly relevant.

The general conclusion reached by the Clinic was that the way in which the event was handled had an observable positive effect and proved the point that copycat suicides need not necessarily follow the suicidal death of a celebrity. Several elements were considered fundamental: the clear distinction drawn by almost all sources between Cobain "the man" and Cobain "the rock star"; little glamorisation of the death (it was clear from reports that he had not simply "drifted" to his death); the participation of Cobain's wife in media events and her portrayal of his death as tragic and wasteful; and the information provided by the Clinic on sources of help that were available.

The concern that suicides may be "encouraged" by the reporting of other cases or imitated as a result of reporting, depending on the details given, is rejected in the publication of the Irish Association of Suicidology's *Media Guidelines on the Portrayal of Suicide* (2000a). These recommendations, while recognising that, understandably, any suicide is newsworthy, media commentators should carry out this reporting in a responsible, sensitive and informed manner. This detailed document covers popular "myths" surrounding suicide (such as "those who talk about suicide are those least likely to do it"), positive examples of the ways in which suicide may be responsibly reported and a list of phrases recommended for use (for example, someone is said to have "died by suicide" rather than "committed suicide", while phrases such as "successful suicide attempt" are strongly advised against so as to avoid the possible glamorisation or promotion of suicidal behaviour). The general aim of this document is to assist the general public and all those involved in the study and reporting of suicidal incidents in coming to a better understanding of this complex issue and to provide accessible, clear language with which this phenomenon may be discussed.

The idea that care is to be taken in the discussion of suicide is not a new one. Leonard (2001) traces the idea that reporting a suicide may play a causal role in additional suicides. While Durkheim in the previously mentioned *Le Suicide* presented the view that only those who wish to take their own lives do so, irrespective of the way in which the event is discussed, others were not as convinced. Leonard cites Parrish (1837) who made the comment that "the publicity which is given to cases of suicide, in the newspapers and by other means, forms one of the strongest incentives to the commission of the act, in those who have a secret disposition to destroy themselves". The popular fiction of the time was also seen to be linked to suicide, with Leonard specifically drawing attention to Charles Dickens' *The Pickwick Papers* containing the following passage (Chapter 23):

> Jist you shut yourself up in your own room, if you've got one, and pison yourself off hand. Hanging's vulgar, so don't you have nothin' to say to that. Pison yourself, Samivel, my boy, pison yourself, and you'll be glad of it afterwards.

Trotter (1807) is also mentioned. Here, the opinion was that fictional suicides were especially "dangerous" in that the fictional world creates a reality which in no way resembles the boundaries and constraints of normal living. Therefore, suicide may be "romantically" or "favourably" presented without the mention of the negative and tragic impact known to accompany real-life suicides.

In more recent times, this approach has come to be recognised as more complex than was previously thought (despite the intuitive appeal of the notion that discussing the behaviour can in reality lead to the carrying out of such behaviour). Hawton (1999) investigated the impact of the dramatic portrayal of a suicide in the BBC drama *Casualty*. This investigation was carried out three weeks pre- and post- screening of the particular episode. Impact was assessed by means of analysis of Accident and

Emergency admissions for overdose by paracetamol (as in the *Casualty* episode) and from other means. It was found that presentations to A&E departments increased by 17 per cent in the week following screening of the episode and by a further 9 per cent two weeks after the episode. Increases in paracetamol overdoses were more marked than overdoses by other means. Thirty-two of the patients who were interviewed (a mere 3 per cent of the total sample) had seen the drama, with 20 per cent of these stating that viewing it had influenced their behaviour and 17 per cent stating that it had specifically influenced their choice of method. Greatest increase was seen in those who matched the gender and age profile of the character shown.

While the authors make the point that such an effect was short-lived, any possibility of reducing the suicide rate is to be welcomed and so, dramatic representations of suicidal behaviours are to be approached with caution. Equally, however, reports of widespread copycat suicides are to be viewed with scepticism. As was seen from the Kurt Cobain case, such a result is by no means inevitable.

One of the more prolific writers on this particular area, Bob Goldney, asserts that while beginning suicide prevention at the level of restricting media images/portrayals etc. of suicide and suicide-related behaviours is intuitively appealing, the link between suicide and its portrayal, although established, is weak at best and preventative action is better taken at the more general level of general health promotion and management. Rather than focus on the possibly negative impact of the media, resources are better spent clarifying the way the media may be used to positive advantage in the dissemination of a positive mental health message (Goldney, 2001).

Cultural Continuity as Suicide Prevention

While our focus thus far has been on social and cultural elements which precede suicidal behaviour, a culture-based model of suicide has yet to be presented. Kazarian and Persad (2001) refer specifically to the process of acculturation and the role it may play in adolescent suicide, alongside other traditionally considered variables (see Figure 4.1).

Figure 4.1: Acculturation and Suicidal Behaviour

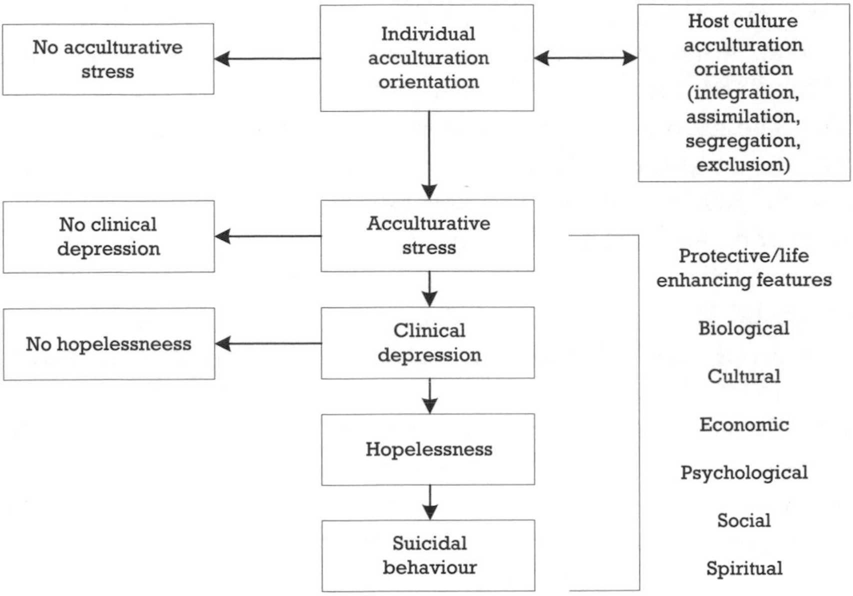

No acculturative stress ← Individual acculturation orientation ↔ Host culture acculturation orientation (integration, assimilation, segregation, exclusion)

Individual acculturation orientation → Acculturative stress

No clinical depression ← Acculturative stress → Clinical depression

No hopelessneess ← Clinical depression → Hopelessness → Suicidal behaviour

Protective/life enhancing features: Biological, Cultural, Economic, Psychological, Social, Spiritual

Source: Kazarian and Persad, 2001

While previous work, such as that of Hovey and King (1996), also looked at acculturation, the experience of acculturative stress which may result and the impact this has on adolescent suicide, it failed to adequately account for different forms of suicidal behaviour, choosing instead to look at suicidal ideation alone.

Kazarian et al. (2001) offer a more inclusive model which seeks to encompass all forms of suicidal behaviour. They also seek to take into account features of culture *independent* of the acculturation strategy of the individual, placing emphasis not only on how the individual will adapt to a new cultural setting but also the way in which the culture will adapt to non-national, immigrant peoples. This is in keeping with what Berry and Kim (1988) term "the nature of the larger society" such that a society which is open to multiculturalism provides a greater degree of tolerance, acceptance of cultural diversity and makes available a socio-cultural network that may help acculturating peoples. In this way, not only is acculturation presented as a multidimensional construct (in keeping with general themes in the literature, see Flannery et al., 2001) but an interdisciplinary approach to suicide is allowed for, thus marking an important step forward, one which is in keeping with our own ideological stance.

The work of Chandler and Lalonde (1998) also sits well within this framework and our own model of *temporal* acculturation. Their work on "cultural continuity" is based on the fundamental assumption that self-continuity has a protective role against suicide. Seeing the self as continuous across time has long been accepted as an essential part of healthy psychological existence (Haber, 1994; Habermas, 1991; Harré, 1979; Rorty, 1976).

Despite the importance of continuity, children are not born with an innate sense of self-continuity across time and so must actively strive to attain and maintain such a sense. Usually, changes in the self which are a normal part of development across the lifespan, from birth to death, occur in a smooth fashion where, despite change, some remnant of one's former self is clearly perceptible. This, however, is not always so during adolescence. Rather, a "cocoon model" of development may be seen, where the adolescent simply "outgrows" their former "skin" and where changes that occur are so dramatic that, for a period, the individual is left without any clear sense of "self". It is at these stages, argue Chandler et al. (1998), that the adolescent is left particularly vulnerable to suicidal behaviour. When one adds to this the context of a changing culture (from which elemental aspects of "self" are derived and through which they may be defined), adolescents in particular are proposed to experience "double jeopardy" risk. Not only are they undergoing extensive personal change, but the external socio-cultural context in which they could "drop anchor" is taken away.

Our own argument is that, just as this applies to geographic culture change (where the cultural location is physically changed), so too does it apply in a situation of temporal acculturation. If their culture-based model is valid, Chandler et al. (1998) assert that several things should follow, most important of which is that adolescents (more than any other age group) should evidence a dramatically elevated rate of suicidal behaviour. Their work is based on First Nations youth in Canada, who are over-represented in the suicide statistics because they evidence the previously mentioned situation of "double jeopardy" risk. We believe that a similar perspective can reasonably be extended to the situation of Irish cultural change.

Finally, Chandler et al. bring the issue of culture into the practical domain with their findings that those cultural groups which have sought "rehabilitation" following change, and which have reinstated many of the traditional and protective cultural practices, have achieved a significant reduction in youth suicide.

We conclude this chapter having moved from implicit examinations of the way in which youth suicide may be influenced by sub-cultural factors to an explicit culture-based model of suicide which offers the possibility of a more grounded and contextually sound model of suicide. What is missing from cultural approaches to suicide is, however, the detail of exactly which factors are influential in a particular cultural setting, and how they interact. Only by fleshing out such details can the preventative value of a cultural approach be realised. We turn our attention to this task in the next and final chapters.

Chapter 5

WHY GENDER?

Razors pain you;
Rivers are damp;
Acids stain you;
And drugs cause cramp;
Guns aren't lawful;
Nooses give;
Gas smells awful;
You might as well live.

— Dorothy Parker (from "Resume")

What is it that increases your chances of ending up in a remedial class at school, in trouble with the police during your adolescence, and in jail by your twenties? What is it that makes you more likely to inject heroin, abuse alcohol, betray your spouse and desert your children? What is it that increases your risk of taking your own and others' lives? The answer: being male (Clare, 2000).

Male suicide has reached epidemic proportions in the "Western" world and especially so in Ireland. Men in Ireland are now nearly four times more likely to die by suicide than their female counterparts. In the first six months of 2002, a total of 199 people died by suicide. Of these, 163 were male CSO.[1] This did not come as any great surprise; we have almost become "used" to the idea that men are more likely to end their own lives. Any consideration of suicide, especially one from a cultural perspective, would therefore be incomplete without

[1] Central Statistics Office — personal communication.

considering its relationship to gender. Being a man in the Ireland of today is evidently no easy task. But *why* is this so? In this chapter we consider traditional understandings of "maleness" and masculinity, how these have changed and how factors such as self-esteem and alcohol consumption are implicated in suicide, particularly in the Irish context.

The Gendering of Suicide

The argument has long been made in critical and developmental circles that the terms "gender" and "sex" are not interchangeable. Gender is socially constructed and will change over time, as will its definition and the meanings ascribed to the term (Ferree, Lorber and Hess, 1999). Sex concerns the "innate structural and physiological characteristics related to reproduction" (Lott and Maluso, 1993, p. 99). It is therefore clear that gender, being about "phenomena and issues related (or assumed to be related) to social and cultural influences . . . is whatever a culture defines and prescribes as feminine and masculine" (Canetto, 1997b). It follows that gender can therefore only be understood from *within* a cultural and social context, independently of which it simply fails to exist in any meaningful way (Ferree et al., 1999).

In much the same way that we have argued that culture has not been meaningfully included in research on suicide, Canetto (1997a) asserts that although gender is frequently mentioned in connection with suicide, research on it is done in the most superficial manner, such that it is examined only as a demographic element, leaving the fundamentals of gendered meaning and context unexplored. Canetto (1997a) also contends that studies that examine non-fatal suicidal behaviours often fail to mention that it is primarily females who are being discussed. Indeed this is now taken for granted. In a similar manner, those studies that concern themselves with completed acts of suicide often fail to mention the predominantly male population involved. In this way, gender has (often) been relegated to the level of the inconsequential — something we already know about. In fact, in reality, little is known about *why* the male rate of suicide has increased while the female rate has remained relatively stable, not just in Ireland but internationally too. One possible reason comes from the social constructionist perspective, which asserts that gender ideologies and socialisation practices vary greatly according to *epoch* and *culture*, such that these differences influence the rates and indeed forms of disorder experienced by men and women (Unger and Crawford, 1996).

Showalter (1997) uses the term *hystories* to describe cultural narratives of hysteria, and includes among her contemporary examples chronic fatigue syndrome, Gulf war syndrome, recovered memories, multiple personality disorder, Satanic ritual abuse and even alien abduction. These conditions (which Showalter sees as psychogenic), it is argued, reflect the anxieties and fantasies of the cultures that harbour them. They may indeed, like their predecessor — hysteria — come to be seen as largely time-bound syndromes, where just as with the more familiar term *culture-bound syndromes*, particular social settings and conditions create certain routes for the expression of distress. These routes change over time, so that while at the turn of the nineteenth/twentieth century we are told that hysterical paralysis was a relatively common ailment, especially among women, now it is very rarely seen. It is our contention that the present settings and conditions in Irish society constitute an epoch that cultivates certain routes for dealing with distress and that for young males, tragically, one of these routes is suicide.

One of the means by which such social settings and conditions may be understood is to consider why it is that more females *engage* in suicidal behaviour but that more males *die as a result of* suicidal behaviour. Canetto (1997b) argues that a good deal of research suggests that in stereotypically "Western" cultures, parasuicidal (i.e. non-fatal suicidal behaviours) acts are inherently seen as "feminine", thus making it "appropriate" for a girl/woman to "attempt" suicide. This is in keeping with the suicide as cry-for-help model. Women, according to this stereotype, do not "mean" to end their lives, they "simply" want attention. Despite the fact that this directly contradicts what is known regarding the motivations of those who behave in a suicidal manner (that is, there is a deeply held desire to escape unbearable distress and torment, discussed in detail in Chapter 4) this stereotypic belief continues to be widely held.

In contrast, it is considered deeply "unmanly" for a boy/man to "cry" for help, and so a suicide "attempt" is less "appropriate" than a completed suicide. Linehan (1973), supporting this gendered distinction, suggests that such stereotypes have long been held. Interestingly, Harry (1983) found that gender role nonconformity during childhood had an impact on later suicidality, such that "feminine" boys were more likely than "masculine" girls to behave in a non-fatal suicidal manner in adulthood, further associating parasuicidal behaviours with femininity (irrespective of biological sex).

In relation to the higher number of males who complete suicide, Canetto (1997b) proposes that there is a certain "draw" towards lethal suicidal behaviours given our (that is, Western) cultural depictions of what it means "to be a man". Thus, men do not "attempt", they "succeed" (note that we have avoided using such terminology previously, as to end one's life is in no way to be deemed a "success", but such language is relevant to the current discussion). As Linehan (1973) puts it, "due to social pressures against attempted suicide, males . . . might 'skip' over the less drastic solution of attempting suicide and go directly to suicide" (p. 32). This same author also notes that individuals who survive a suicide attempt are rated as less masculine than those whose lives end as a result of suicidal behaviour.

Non-fatal suicidal behaviours are, it would seem, generally seen as violations of the stereotypical "male" role expectations that include the attributes of strength, decisiveness, success and *in*expressiveness. Not only may such expectations impede men from openly expressing hopelessness, despair, depression and isolation (a problem in itself) but when behaving to alleviate these experiences, the selection of method is also affected. One of the most disturbing findings in this vein was reported by Lewis and Shepeard (1992), who found that men who ended their lives as a result of suicidal behaviour were thought to be more "well-adjusted" than women who behaved in the same manner — in short, to behave in a suicidal manner is "manly" and therefore not "abnormal" and even "acceptable" in certain circumstances within this cultural depiction of masculinity. The fact that fatal suicidal behaviour and adjustment have ever been coupled is surely concerning. Ellis and Range (1988) summarise that "the traditional development of masculine sex roles in our society is not adaptive in terms of facilitating an individual's belief which would prevent suicide" (p. 299).

We suspect that the "inexpressiveness" of some young men may be a key factor in their greater propensity to suicide. Is it that men, because of their socialisation in our society, do not feel comfortable with communicating their distress to others? Or is it that, again because of their socialisation in our society, they have never learned to identify *when* or in fact *how* to communicate distress? We will return to these issues in the final chapter.

WHITHER "MAN"?

Often, considerations of the decline of the modern man into distress, dysfunction and despair begin with a review of the feminist movement. This argument may be paraphrased as follows: women, by asserting their equality and actively working against being classed as second-class citizens, through the organisation of feminism, are "responsible" for the current male "situation" and have somehow "caused" men to become depressed, alcoholic, violent or suicidal. Male power is being overthrown and, like colonists seeing their empire crumble, men don't like what is happening and look to feminism for a defensive explanation. However, as we gradually come to recognise the complexities of the influence of gender, we also realise that to cast feminism as simply an opposition to men is too simplistic. Furthermore, although feminism has achieved much for women in the realm of equality and opportunity, it is also apparent that men continue to occupy positions of power, continue to earn more on average and hold fast to their higher status. Women continue to be their children's primary caregivers, even when working outside the home, thus allowing the gender disparity in unpaid labour to continue.

To consider the situation of modern men and women in these terms alone, however, is to completely miss the point. Men have not simply been "overthrown" at the hands of "feminist women"; rather, the very existence of men, their purpose, their *raison d'être*, is being fundamentally questioned and continually challenged. The very meaning of "man" is in disarray and the value of patriarchy is perched precariously on the technological cliff tops that have given us IVF, cloning and the capacity for women to procreate without the suspicion of male genitalia, or the men attached to the sperm involved (MacLachlan, 2003b). This, of course, can result in a great deal of male insecurity and possibly an aggressive response against both others and themselves. Apart from being made inert, technologically redundant and socially sterile, our image of maleness has become increasingly negative: they are the abusers, the rapists, the paedophiles, the alcoholics . . . the suicidal.

This was not always the case, however. A century ago, to be a man meant to be a leader in public life, a patriarch at home; being male was the very definition of health and maturity. The definition of "successful man" did not merely embody the characteristics of decisiveness, rationality, calmness, discipline, resourcefulness. "Maleness" was also defined in terms of what it was *not* — that is, fragility, weakness, vulnerability, emotionality, impetuousness, dependence, nervousness — the stereotype of the "weaker sex". Today's man is cast as a shadow of the manhood which, while forged over a number of centuries, came into its own in the nineteenth century, a century of unparalleled male achievement in science, technology, biology, medicine, exploration and imperial expansion. When the inheritance of man is discussed, it is not merely his genes or his biological destiny that is being referred to, but the social expectations, the cultural notions of what it means to be "man". The men of previous times were in control. Today, men are in confusion. When it comes to work, procreation, family and so many other areas of life, women can perform *as well as* men, *even in the absence of men*. There is little left that is uniquely male and even less that exclusively defines that which is "masculine".

Looking to the family, traditionally, a man was "king of his castle"; whatever challenges or threats he faced in public life, when he returned home to his family, his position was clear. He was master of the household, head of the *clan*. The decline of the traditional nuclear family represents one of the less recognised, but arguably the most significant, of all the threats to male "superiority". The death of the patriarch is not just an important structural change in the long evolution of social and family relationships. The decline of the two-parent family and the rise in the number of families headed by women creates the very antithesis of the patriarchal family. Where once the family was dominated by an adult male, now in more and more families there is no longer an adult male to be seen, much less one who is in sole control.

Historically, we became so accustomed to the gendering of the public and private spheres, of men earning their reputation and deriving their self-esteem from the public sphere and of women confined and assessed within the private, that we may now be in danger of underestimating the relationship between masculinity and domesticity. Much of the self-esteem which men possess, perhaps most of it, has derived from the reputation *outside* the home, earned in making a living, engaging in a profession, changing the world. Historical scholarship, sociological research and psychological theorising have all contributed to the notion that, until recently, the public sphere has *belonged* to men. The underlying assumption that has been so omnipresent is that what makes (or indeed, breaks) a man is what he does *outside of the home*. Yet, clearly, the division between public and private spheres has never been absolute — a man's duty to his family has also been a fundamental part of his masculinity and self-respect. The man who was not master in his own house earned the derision and ridicule of his peers and society more generally, and the extent to which his personal life and most intimate relationships were either disciplined or chaotic affected the way he was perceived and judged. *This* was also a measure of his character, his worth. The traditional model of the family required the male head of the house, the father, the husband, to over-rule women in decision-making, to discipline his children and provide a model for decent "upstanding" living to others. Social and cultural traditions meant that most adult men expected to become husbands and fathers (thus taking up these roles and the responsibilities). The average couple was expected to have eight children surviving past infancy, and often a man was over 60 before his youngest child married and left home (Clare, 2000). Thus, the job of husband and father was not only substantive in determining one's worth but was also a lifelong task.

By the latter half of the nineteenth century, the growth of what continues to be a particular problem of modern family life — the separation of home from work and, with it, the beginnings of the isolation and diminution of fatherhood — was well under way. The nineteenth century was the first in which significant numbers of men of education and means began to experience work as alienating because of the polluted environment in which they had to do it and the dehumanised personal relationships which characterised it (Tosh, 1999). The technological and economic progress of the industrial revolution was brought at an appalling cost. One consequence was the separation of the place of work from the place of residence, which perhaps led to the home becoming in men's eyes a refuge of psychological and emotional support.

The problem, however, was that while the nineteenth century patriarch might regularly retreat to his home for rest and emotional sustenance, he could no longer hope to exercise unquestioned authority within it. For one thing, he was only at home for relatively short periods. Apart from his workplace, there were the alternative attractions of all-male clubs, all-male sports and the burgeoning array of associations and community groups which helped divert men from a potentially greater involvement with domestic responsibilities. On both sides of the Atlantic, the power within the home began to shift from father to mother (Demos, 1986). In the first half of the nineteenth century, fathers were given the largest share of blame or credit for how their children developed and generally "turned out", they had more frequent contact with their adolescent and adult children and played a central role in the cycle and existence of the family. By the end of the nineteenth century, however, the mother's role in the domestic framework had become pre-eminent. As early as 1847, a New York court had declared that "all other things being equal, the mother is the most proper person to be entrusted with the custody of the child", and by the end of the century the law, at one with common opinion, "affirmed maternal pre-eminence in childrearing" (Demos, 1986, p. 57).

In a similar vein, the Irish Constitution reserves a special place for the mother within the family; thus, although divorce only became a reality much later here, there was a broad mirroring of this policy in Ireland. By the turn of the twentieth century, men had lost their former place in the home — it was now the mother who acted as child adviser, moral guide and decision-maker and, gradually, the belief that men had (nor ought to have, given their "disposition" and "nature") little or no part in the nurturing of children, took firm root. Perhaps this withdrawal from the home is just one of the many sources of support and personal meaning that has been lost to men, so putting them in self-harm's way.

One of the key issues both in suicide research and clinical practice is the evaluation and identification of those who may be at risk of behaving in a suicidal manner. Traditionally, it was thought that the best predictor of suicidal behaviour was an individual's level of hopelessness, that is, the degree to which they held negative thoughts and expectations. This line of thinking originated with the clinical work of Aaron Beck (1963, 1967) who proposed that it was the cognitive feature of hopelessness which was central to the experience of suicide. While people may experience both depression and hopelessness, according to this model the effects of the former far outweigh the latter and, on this basis, the Beck Hopelessness Scale was devised. Much of the work carried out in the investigation of this theory was done with an adult population, most of whom were in clinical settings, leaving the relationship between hopelessness, depression and adolescent suicide unexamined for the most part.

Cole (1989) specifically researched this question, reasoning that if the Beck model holds good explanatory power for youth suicide, then hopelessness measures should correlate better with measures of suicidal ideation and behaviour than any other measure of psychological experience. When this was tested, however, the relationships which emerged were far more complex than had previously been thought. The most interesting finding was that *gender-dependent paths to suicide* emerged strongly. For boys, the experience of hopelessness was a less significant indicator of suicidal thoughts and behaviours than depression (contrary to Beck's original hypothesis), but for girls, the importance of the hopelessness component remained, even when depression was controlled for.

On this basis, and given our current level of understanding of the multiple and varied experiences that lead a young person to the point of suicide, we may conclude that *both* depression and hopelessness need to be assessed. To disregard one is to fail to fully examine the situation and allows risk to go undetected. This is in keeping with the more recent recommendations of Kumar and Steer (1995) that measures of hopelessness and depression, when used in conjunction in an assessment/research setting are the most powerful predictors of suicidal ideation. It is, however, also important to note (as Beck himself did) that use of such screening tools alone is insufficient to adequately and successfully address the issue of youth suicide. While clinical measures such as these offer a "snapshot" of the individual's experience and psychological state, additional prevention and education programmes are of course necessary.

Male Risk

Suicide is between two and five times more common in men than in women in Europe, North America, Africa and Latin America. In Britain, there are approximately 6,000 suicides each year — one every 85 minutes. The rates of male suicide in all age groups and in most countries have shown a striking increase over the past 30 years with the most dramatic increase to be seen in those aged fifteen to twenty-four years. Although, traditionally, suicide rates increased with age, recent times have seen youth suicides come to outnumber elderly suicides (Clare, 2000). In most European countries, men account for about three-quarters of the people who kill themselves. These same patterns are to be seen in Ireland. Equally noteworthy is the fact that despite this increase in male suicide, the female suicide rate has remained relatively stable, perhaps suggesting that those socio-cultural factors which influence suicide differentially affect males and females (see Figures 5.1, 5.2 and 5.3).

Figure 5.1: Number of Suicides in Ireland

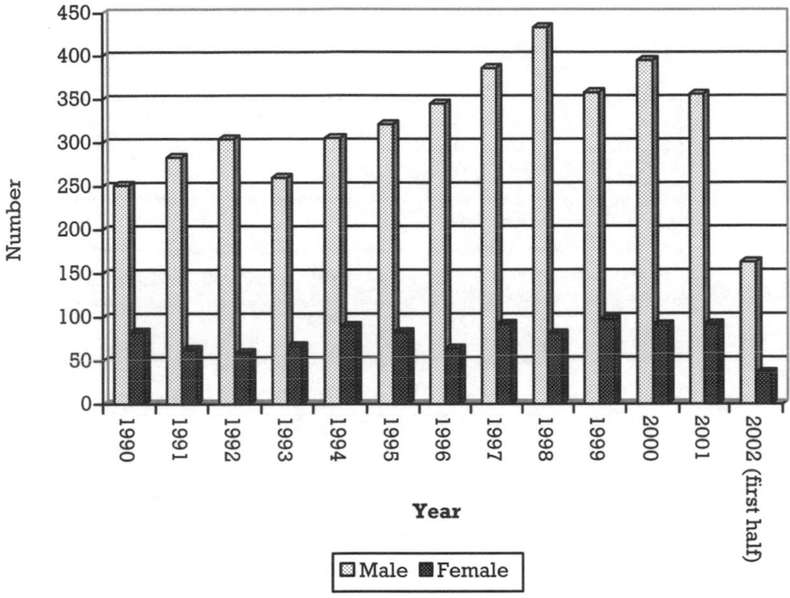

Figure 5.2: Youth versus Elderly Male Suicide

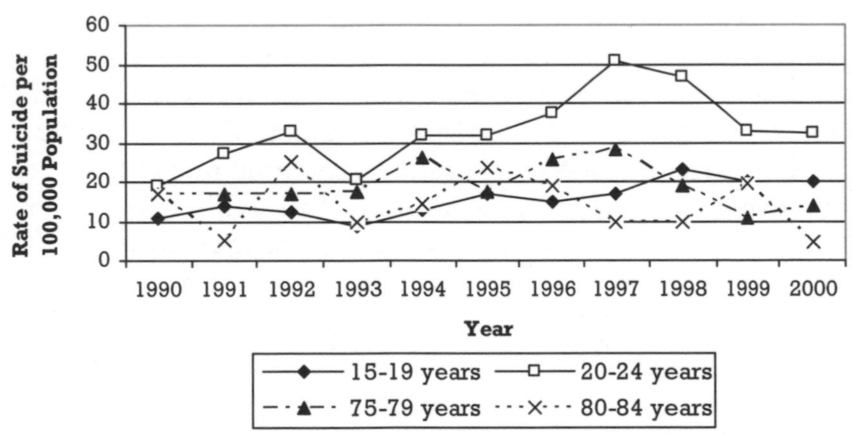

Figure 5.3: Youth versus Elderly Female Suicide

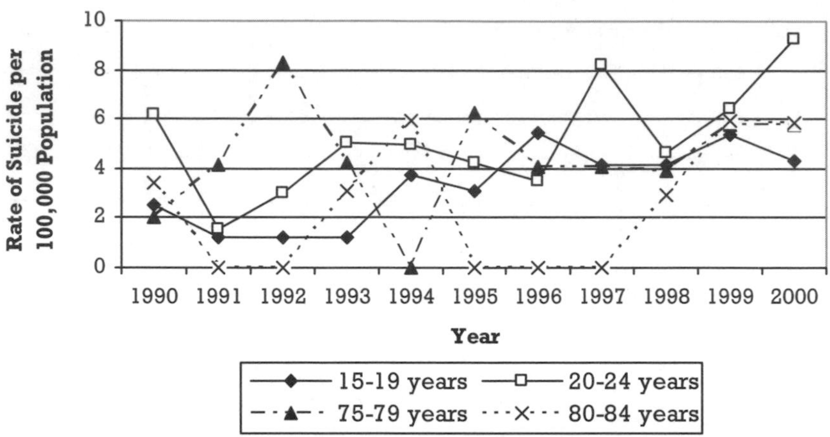

Suicide in men has been linked to each of depression (Isometsa et al., 1995), alcohol abuse (Lesage et al., 1994) and drug abuse (Rich, Young and Fowler, 1986) among other factors. Looking specifically at the role alcohol has come to play in our society, a recent article in *The Irish Times* (21 September 2002) asserts that three out of ten fifteen-year-olds drink with the specific intention of getting drunk. While ten of the European Union member states (among them, Italy, Belgium and Sweden) have witnessed a decrease in alcohol consumption in the years 1989 to 1999, Ireland has seen a 41 per cent increase in alcohol consumption during this same period, to the point that our per capita alcohol consumption rate (which is currently 11.1 pure litres of alcohol per person in contrast to the European average of 9.1 litres) is exceeded only by Luxembourg (see Figure 4.4). This figure of 11.1 litres may however give a distorted impression of the actual increase we have seen in this ten-year period. When adult consumption levels alone are examined (given that children under the age of 15 are predominantly non-drinkers) the annual rate of consumption per person increases to 14.2 litres. When the specific type of alcohol being consumed was examined, it was seen that sales of spirits increased by 10 per cent in 1996 with this trend continuing to the present. Much of this increase may be explained by the "new generation" of alco-pops and drinks aimed primarily at a youth market (Department of Health and Children, 2002).

Figure 5.4: Change in Alcohol Consumption, 1989–2000

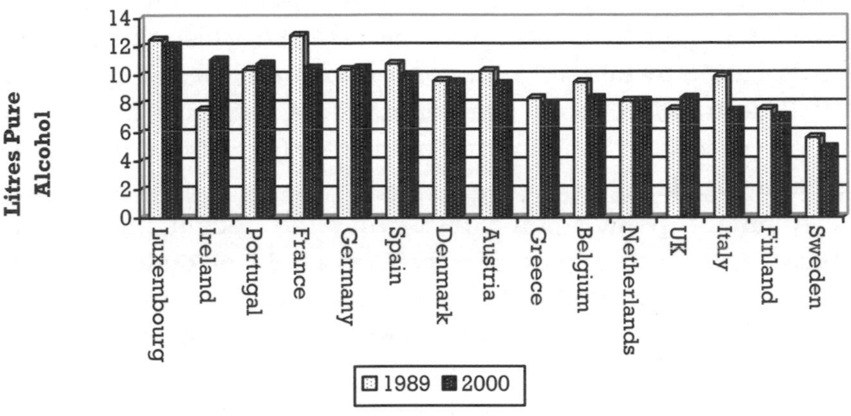

While experimentation with alcohol (and indeed other, often illegal, substances) may be considered a normative part of adolescence, some findings suggest that by the time Ireland's teenagers reach the age of fifteen, half the girls and nearly two-thirds of the boys may be classed as "current drinkers" with one-third of this group reporting "binge drinking" (defined as having five or more drinks in a row) three or more times in the last month (Hibell et al., 2000).

The Department of Health's interim report on alcohol (2002) also draws attention to the societal impact of such an increase in alcohol consumption by examining each of unintentional injuries/accidents, personal relationships, interpersonal violence/public safety, drink driving, alcohol-related mortality, mental health problems and economic cost of alcohol-related problems, stating that none go unaffected by the rise in alcohol use and abuse that has been seen.

With specific regard to mental health, the report states that "alcohol abuse is a significant risk factor in suicide and *compounds the other factors* . . ." (Department of Health, 2002, p. 11, italics added). In keeping with the cultural model presented here, we believe this adequately summarises the complex relationship — while alcohol consumption may indeed reduce inhibition and, by this means, increase the risk of suicide, it is not in and of itself a causal factor, but is to be better understood as a maladaptive, (often) socially sanctioned and legally condoned coping mechanism which exists within our culture. Thus alcohol consumption may precipitate a suicidal attempt, rather than being a reason for it. At the same time, we recognise that chronic alcohol use may interact with depression and low self-esteem in a self-destructive spiral that reinforces a person's feelings of hopelessness and despair, and ultimately leads them to attempt to end their life.

A further point when considering the recent increase in young, male suicide specifically is the role of biology, especially when we consider the emphasis that has been placed on biomedical explanations for the suicide phenomenon in recent times.

Kraemer (2000) makes an interesting observation on the relationship between male behaviour and biological makeup:

> the human male is, on most measures, more vulnerable than the female. Part of the explanation is the biological fragility of the male fetus, which is little understood and not widely known. A typical attitude to boys is that they are, or must be made, more resilient than girls. This adds social insult to biological injury. Culture and class make a difference to the health and survival of boys (p. 1609).

From this statement alone, written by someone within the biomedical tradition, it is clear that the "problem" of "maleness" cannot rest in biology alone. While biological aspects without doubt play a key role at the point of conception, *in utero* development and birth, beyond this, it is those social and cultural factors which take a more dominant role. Kraemer asserts that the pre-existing "condition" of maleness, if you will, may thus be exacerbated or alleviated by the social and cultural conditions in which that male exists. Through the socialisation process, the cultural value or status differentially afforded to males and females and the genderised expectations of those surrounding the male, the very way in which a man can "be" is affected. Perhaps one of the greatest, and only recently discussed, risks to males is their lack of emotional expression. Boys who don't talk, who become ashamed of their emotions and, indeed, become ashamed of being ashamed, who try to stop themselves feeling anything, thus seeming invulnerable to themselves and others, are those for whom the experience of "maleness" is most perilous.

Clare (2000), in the same vein, examines the role which hormones, specifically male hormones, have in determining human behaviour. He argues that while the animal research evidence is certainly useful in assisting our understanding of human behaviour, when this research is extended to encompass human behaviour and given causal significance, some of the findings presented are over-reaching and provide a truly biased view of the role of biology. We will now examine some of the examples Clare provides.

Medical history itself offers us the opportunity to investigate the role of the male hormone, *testosterone*. Between the 1940s and 1970s, over half a million pregnant women were treated with the drug *diethylbestrol* (DES) to prevent the spontaneous abortion of fetuses in pregnancies at risk of miscarriage. The effects of DES are similar (in animals) to the effects of male hormones. Thus, if animal research findings were to hold for human behaviour, we would expect that female fetuses exposed to DES would behave in a "masculine" way. When 30 DES-exposed women were compared with 30 non-exposed women, results were generally inconclusive and provided only the *suggestion* of increased "male" behaviour (Ehrhardt et al., 1989). This presumed "male" behaviour was, however, related to the poorer parenting skills of DES-affected women and offers us greater insight into the stereotypical expectations regarding men's ability to parent than it does the role of hormones on human behaviour.

Another possible source of information comes from where the production of abnormally large amounts of the male hormone androgens is seen in genetically affected females. Women experiencing this condition have a genotypic structure of XX (as in the case of unaffected females) but as a result of the high levels of androgens, experience a masculisation of their genitalia at birth. If left untreated, these individuals manifest a masculine physical appearance, a deepening of the voice, an enlarged clitoris and a lack of breast development at puberty. Some studies on the impact of CAH (congenital adrenal hyperplasia) (for example, Berenbaum and Hynes, 1992) showed that affected girls behaved in a more "tomboyish" manner in their childhood years and focused on career rather than child-rearing fantasies for their futures (again, note that focus on career was taken as an indication of maleness). While superficially, affected girls may appear to behave in stereotypically "male" ways, the number of girls affected by this condition is small and one of the key aspects many fail to mention is that girls experiencing this condition are both psychologically and anatomically seriously affected. Until surgery takes place, the enlarged clitoris appears penis-like and they appear to have a scrotum. Furthermore, studies such as this fail to make reference to the fundamental processes of parental expectation and socialisation (whereby girls who appear to be boys may elicit boy-related expectations from their parents). At best, this type of research leaves the situation entirely unclear; at worst it presents an inaccurate portrayal of the way in which biology exerts its effect.

As Clare (2000) points out, there is something fundamentally attractive about this level of analysis of contemporary problems. If we are to attribute the causes of these complex behaviours to linear, biomedical processes, it makes them far easier to discuss, for we are no longer trying to restructure a society's culture (those grey areas which are inherently complex and are often seen as too problematic for inclusion in considerations) but instead are looking at something capable of being "fixed" in the tradition of the biomedical approach. Perhaps this is why, even in the face of contradictory evidence, these theories are held so dear.

Not only does such a perspective underestimate the role played by social and cultural factors, but it portrays men as mere puppets, ruled by their genetic make-up and their hormonal functioning. It leaves little freedom to be, to change and to break free of the negative stereotypes that exist. This neither does justice to our level of understanding of human behaviour nor to men as self-determined individuals.

Reconsidering Masculinity?

While woman report higher rates of mental health problems in general, as we have seen, young males in particular are more likely to end their lives through suicide. In recognition of this, and that being male in the Ireland of today is problematic, the Department of Education and Science produced the *Exploring Masculinities* (2000) programme. This programme is intended for use with transition year and senior cycle boys.

In introducing this programme, it is stated that

> The last quarter of the twentieth century has seen profound changes in Irish society. Many of these changes have received extensive publicity, i.e. the onset of the information society, the impact of the scientific and technological world, and the internationalisation of the economy. . . . Paradoxically, this progress that is designed to create a better life for all is matched by a sense of fear in many, which change frequently engenders. . . . The social, psychological and emotional consequences of such rapid change have not been given similar publicity and have not been addressed to the extent that is necessary for many. These changes are not without difficulties, but little attention has been paid to how individuals are coping or are being prepared to cope with them (pp. *v–vii*).

These statements are commendable and reflect a clear recognition that the cultural, social and psychological impacts of change demand our careful attention and analysis. Sadly, however, and perhaps as a reflection of a society ambivalent about the consequences of its changing, the *Exploring Masculinities* programme has been a focus of some controversy. To get an impression of the extent of use of the programme, we conducted a brief "phone-around" survey of some twenty post-primary schools in the Dublin area, chosen at random from the telephone book. We simply asked if they were using the *Exploring Masculinities* programme, and if not, what the reasoning behind their decision was. *Not one* of the twenty schools we contacted was using the programme. Reasons were given for this included a complete lack of awareness of the existence of the programme (one of the most memorable remarks in response to the name was "Exploring *what*? Jaysus! . . ."), a feeling that it was exclusionary to girls in a mixed setting (for both principled and practical reasons — principled, in that many felt that the issue of gender and masculinity was best explored in a setting open to *both* males and females, and practical in that those mixed schools did not have the resources to segregate classes in order to implement the programme — a concern regarding some of the material on sexual orientation (that the programme required the discussion of sexuality at all, and that the very mention of homosexuality may "induce" the "condition" — neither of which was felt to be desirable) and a lack of teacher resources. It is important to note that some of these concerns (such as lack of teacher support) were mentioned in the independent evaluation of the programme carried out at time of publication and so are clearly already known (Gleeson, 1999).

Clearly these issues should be of concern to us — yes, to *all* of us. Furthermore, we understand that the Department of Education and Science has, at present, no systematic manner of promoting the programme to schools and that it appears to operate an informal "don't ask, don't tell" policy with regard to its implementation, as no examination of the rate of uptake of the programme has taken place to date. The Department of Education and Science apparently feels that given the "sensitive" nature of the programme, specific training would be required for its implementation, especially when one considers the "widespread feelings of homophobia among boys". When asked if there was concern over the apparent low uptake and feeling that it excluded girls, we were informed that the programme was intended to be used in conjunction with the earlier *Balance: Who Cares?* (1997) programme, thought to redress any imbalance. It is of course frustrating and quite inappropriate that we can only cite "off-the-record" remarks given by a person within the Department of Education, when such an issue should be publicly debated and facilitated at the behest of the same government department.

The rationale given for the development of the *Balance: Who Cares?* module available to post-primary schools is

> to explore and discuss issues of gender equality relating to the sharing of domestic work, equality in the workplace and the sharing of community work. . . . The overall aim of the module is to enable young people to think about their futures in a structured way and to examine critically their expectations and life plans . . ." (p. *x*).

Interestingly, it has also been suggested to us — again "off-the-record" — that there was a general feeling that the *Balance* programme was (ironically) "too girly", thus explaining the need for the *Exploring Masculinities* programme. This is despite the fact that the *Balance* programme is pitched as much to boys as to girls, with examples provided for both genders, thus not precluding its use in a single-sex boys' setting.

The National Council for Curriculum and Assessment (NCCA) carried out a final review of the *Exploring Masculinities* programme (National Council for Curriculum and Assessment, 2002). Before presenting a brief summary of some of these findings, however, it is important to note that in addition to this research, an external evaluation of *Exploring Masculinities* was carried out by Jim Gleeson of the University of Limerick. Despite numerous and repeated requests and despite the fact that the NCCA's own report relies heavily on selected parts of Dr Gleeson's work, this external research remains, as yet, unpublished. And so, while *some* information is available on issues relating to the *Exploring Masculinities* programme generally, much information has failed to successfully make its way to the public domain. We trust then that readers can draw their own conclusions on this basis.

The opening section of the NCCA report addresses the rationale for the commissioning of this research. The Education Act (1998) calls for the NCCA to occasionally carry out curriculum reviews on behalf of the Minister for Education. Given the media attention surrounding the *Exploring Masculinities* programme for schools, it was felt that NCCA involvement in the review was required with discussion of each of the following: *Exploring Masculinities* materials; current status of the programme in schools; summary of the public debate surrounding *Exploring Masculinities*; examination of teacher's classroom practices; and conclusions and recommendations for the future of *Exploring Masculinities*.

With regard to professional development for those teachers participating in the teaching of *Exploring Masculinities*, a four-stage plan was developed for the dissemination of information relating to the teaching of the programme in schools. The proposed structure of this training included the following elements: one full day of in-service training for teachers of senior cycle students who wished to implement either the *Balance* or *Exploring Masculinities* programmes; plans for ongoing support of teachers involved in the teaching of these programmes; and the establishment of local clusters of teachers engaged with this material at a local level. Only some of the initial phase of training took place as a result of ASTI industrial action and the practical issues raised by the foot-and-mouth outbreak. Schools in the Mid-West, Midlands North-West and Dublin participated in the training phase. *No* schools from the South or South-East had any introduction to the programme and *none* of the subsequent phases of training took place (p. 16).

To assess the status of *Exploring Masculinities* in schools (at the time of publication of the NCCA report) a survey of schools was carried out between November 2001 and January 2002. Schools were sent two questionnaires — one in the event they were teaching *Exploring Masculinities* (which would be passed on to the teacher/teachers responsible) and one for those not teaching the programme to be filled out by principals and addressed reasons for lack of implementation. The authors clearly state that the development of these questionnaires was based on their reading and interpretation of the "Limerick Evaluation" and so the specific methodological development and theoretical foundations of the questionnaire materials remains unclear. The questionnaires were mailed to single-sex boys' schools (irrespective of whether or not they had a TY programme). No clear information on the number of schools initially contacted is provided but a statement that "all 120 boys' single-sex schools were surveyed" (p. 35) is made. Of these, 32 returned questionnaires, and of these 32 only fourteen were teaching *Exploring Masculinities* (in relation to the fourteen, *Exploring Masculinities* may not still be in place, as this figure included schools who had at one point, but may no longer be, teaching the course).

When the comments made by those teachers using *Exploring Masculinities* were explored, various reasons for its introduction became apparent. These ranged from concerns over the increase in young, male suicide to a need for the gender issue to be explored (this latter point was made with reference to co-ed settings where this issue was felt to be more salient, perhaps indicating a problem with *Exploring Masculinities* being aimed primarily at single-sex settings).

The authors reach the conclusion that whether or not teachers were *actually* teaching *Exploring Masculinities*, there was strong support for the programme on the basis of the finding that 94 per cent of the returned questionnaires either strongly agreed or agreed that there was a need for a programme which allowed boys to discuss personal, social or health issues. It was *not stated*, however, that this 94 per cent felt that *Exploring Masculinities* was the *best* way to do this, and given the low rate of actual programme usage (not addressed by the report), it could perhaps be concluded that while there is support for programmes such as this *in theory*, when it comes to implementation, support wanes.

When questionnaire responses from those *not* using the programme were examined, various concerns were raised. These included a feeling that the ethos of the programme and that of the school were poorly matched (no additional detail on this is provided) and that the controversy in various forms of media were off-putting — the programme was not worth the hassle. Some schools which had previously taught *Exploring Masculinities* but subsequently discontinued the programme raised ideological concerns as their reason — this was referred to as insignificant by the authors and not examined in greater detail, leaving some confusion as to the exact nature of the ideological concern. Interestingly, in schools where *Exploring Masculinities* was being taught, equal numbers of male and female teachers were involved (thus the concern that it was primarily women indoctrinating boys, as raised by the media, appears unfounded). Of the fourteen schools engaged with *Exploring Masculinities*, *none* taught the programme in its entirety, with a "sampling approach" favoured (that is, some of the sections would be used but others were left out completely). From the descriptive statistics provided, it appears that elements of the sections on "Men and Power", "Relationships, health and sexuality" and "Violence against women, men and children" were those left out. (See Table 5.1 for a summary of the topics in the programme.)

Table 5.1: Summary of Topics from Educational Programme* Exploring Masculinities *(2000)

Theme	Section Heading	Example of Issues Included
Theme 1	*Starting Out*	Learning in a safe environment The Freedom To Be
Theme 2	*Men Working*	The Equality Debate My Ideal Job Work In The Home
Theme 3	*Men and Power*	Defining Bullying I Know Tim's Number By Heart (bullying in the context of intimate relationships) Strategies For Coping With Bullying
Theme 4	*Relationships, Health and Sexuality*	Talking Sex Sexual Myths Understanding Gay People
Theme 5	*Violence Against Women, Men and Children*	Feeling Safe, Feeling Fear The Cycle of Domestic Violence Violence Against Children — sexual abuse
Theme 6	*Men and Sport*	Scoring in Sport The Dressing Rooms The Winner Takes It All
Theme 7	*Wrapping It Up*	Images of Man We Can Work It Out

While the authors readily conclude that teachers are "overwhelmingly supportive" of the programme (whether or not they teach it), it is unclear as to how this conclusion is reached on the basis of the descriptive statistics provided and certainly given the low response rate generally, and the low rate of programme usage. Typically, those schools which use *Exploring Masculinities* are urban or town-based rather than rural. *Why* this might be so and *how* this imbalance may be redressed was not addressed.

While these programmes (i.e. *Exploring Masculinities* and *Balance: Who Cares?*) have been created with good intention and appear to represent a proactive and progressive approach (in Irish terms at least, but by no means progressive when other European nations are considered), in practice they appear to receive little more than lip service. Scant support is given to teachers who are already under immense pressure and who often work in less than ideal conditions in an education setting which in practice places almost total emphasis on academic success and scholastic achievement. While we would not wish to suggest that the Department of Education and Science desire to *appear* to be considering these issues but are in fact only paying *lip-service* to them, others may be drawn to this conclusion.

Despite the fact that Ireland's suicide problem is considerable and that concerns over this and other mental health issues are regularly raised in public forums, there continues to be an unwillingness to openly engage with and publicly think through controversial issues. The Department of Education and Science is not alone in this, however. Perhaps the clearest example of this is the legal case taken by one parent in response to the aforementioned *Exploring Masculinities* programme. The story was initially reported in *The Irish Times* by education correspondent Emmet Oliver (8 March 2001). The father of a fourteen-year-old secondary school student (who, it should be noted, would not at this age have been eligible to participate), attempted to make a constitutional challenge to the programme on the grounds that it violated Article 42 of the Constitution which recognises the family as the "primary and natural" educator of children. This case was later withdrawn with Mr Patrick Brennan of the Department of Education and Science's legal section stating that:

> The materials developed by the Department of Education and Science are made available to all post-primary schools,

> whether the schools use the programme or parts of it is a matter for each board of management. Section 30 of the Education Act, 1998 ensures that parents have the right to withdraw their children from any course of study to which they object. Whereas the Education (Welfare) Act, 2000 requires children to be in education at least until 16 years of age, Art 42(3) of the constitution provides that parents may provide education in the home rather than send their child to a school (personal communication, 2002).

As we have maintained throughout, suicide is not mystically induced by the mere mention of the word. Rather, a complex series of social, cultural, psychological and biological factors converge to result in this phenomenon. We will *not* reduce the suicide rate generally, nor prevent individual acts of suicide or self-harm, by banishing this as a topic for open, frank discussion. A sense of isolation and a feeling that one is not understood or heard at a time of great emotional and psychological suffering (the oft-mentioned *psychache*) is the most commonly cited "reason" for suicide (Shneidman, 1985). Our culture has for too long been complicit through its silence on suicide. It is time to change that as well. The confusion, fear and general unease that surround the *Exploring Masculinities* programme can be taken as an indication of where we, as a society "are at", and generally, the picture isn't good.

In the programmes *Exploring Masculinities* and *Balance: Who Cares?* there exists a starting point (admittedly, not perfect but a benchmark nonetheless) for a mental health promotion programme in Ireland's secondary schools. Certainly, the elements which address roles in society, emotional expression and relationships and the issue of violence/bullying could serve as useful discussion points which directly relate to the aforementioned and problematic areas of male emotional expression, coping and, perhaps ultimately, suicidal risk. However, for as long as the high levels of discomfort, confusion and general reluctance surround these programmes, *any* attempt at school-based suicide prevention is hindered. In the last chapter we will go on to examine possible preventions and consider the way in which we might go forward.

Chapter 6

WHY SUICIDE?

Some factors that influence suicidal behaviour are macro-environmental, and can be manipulated through government policy (socio-economic issues, poverty, racism, housing, employment, income and education). Some in turn are micro-environmental and influenced by the individual . . . [family and community] . . . (mental health; self-esteem; depression; substance abuse; physical, emotional and sexual abuse; familial factors; life events; and negative authoritative involvement). *Culture moves between both of these arenas, and is difficult and dynamic to quantify in association with . . . suicide* (Coupe, 2002, pp. 59–60, *italics added*).

. . . it sometimes seems that young people are engaged in a tussle between hope and cynicism, aimed at warding off disappointment . . . the cultural focus of the individual "self" has weakened social cohesion, undermined the sense of belonging, and left the "self" dangerously exposed and isolated (Eckersley, 1997, p. 423).

TOWARDS PREVENTION

In this book we have described suicide in historical and cultural perspectives and outlined some salient factors that we believe strongly relate to its occurrence. We have asked three key questions: Why culture? Why youth? Why gender? Simple questions to ask, but undoubtedly multifaceted and complex to answer. In this chapter, we think through the implications, for the prevention of suicide, of the arguments we have made. We construct a schematic that portrays the interrelationship of various salient cultural factors and we point up some strategies that should be acted on. We also caution that no schematic, framework or model can be all-encompassing and that even though we emphasise the importance of cultural factors, we recognise that people are not "cultural dopes", simply following the paths of socialisation laid down by others. However, the inevitable individual variation in how people respond to cultural forces does not exonerate either our individual or collective responsibility for trying to shape a society that cultivates good health, self-respect and realistic alternatives to suicide.

While people may not be "cultural dopes" nor are they "social islands". Personal well-being is not only multidimensional in the sense of it being constructed of many different domains of life, it is also hierarchical, in the sense that it is influenced by the well-being of the family, which in turn is influenced by the well-being of the community, and further by the well-being of society (Prilleltensky and Nelson, 2002). However, the term "society" is ambiguous in a modern world with a myriad of internet, television and media interconnections that entwine our now small globe. Today few societies encapsulate; most simply filter outside influences through their own socially constructed web of meaning and in doing so imbue some special sense of what it is to be in the world as an Irish person, or German person, or whatever.

A Schematic of Suicide

Figure 6.1 seeks to summarise some of the factors that we believe are responsible for suicides in Ireland, particularly in young men. The schematic (or way of representing the idea) is primarily concerned with "ultimate" causes rather than proximate ones (that is, immediate causes, such as hopelessness, depression, which we see as usually being reactions to distressing circumstances). The schematic therefore tries to explicate the settings and conditions that make the occurrence of proximate causes of suicide more likely. The model places the individual at the centre, and as we spiral outward and upward, it represents other layers of influence in the individual's life. Some models that seek to convey the relationship between the individual and other facets of society, place the individual at the top of a pyramid (e.g. Prilleltensky and Nelson, 2002), but we feel that this representation fails to capture the powerful influence that other psychological, social and cultural factors have on the individual, often conspiring to leave a very limited range of actions available for people in a given situation. We feel that this sense of "constraint" is better captured by a figure that deepens inward.

Our schematic representation therefore has the appearance of a filter, or funnel, but it is also the case that each layer of influence may be filtered through those below it. Thus, global culture influences Irish society, which in turn influences local communities, which in turn has an influence on the families within it, which also have influence over their individual members. However, as everyone knows, and as every parent fears, globalisation also takes a very direct route — by-passing Irish society, community and family — directly into our children's bedrooms through their TV, internet connections, magazines and so on. Thus, while each of the levels in our hierarchy may be filtered through the influence of the one below it, in an information age we are each capable of reaching into and being reached by, any one of these levels, in its "pure form". One insufficiently recognised consequence of this is that any two individuals within the same family may be identifying themselves with radically different "virtual" communities and effectively living in quite different worlds.

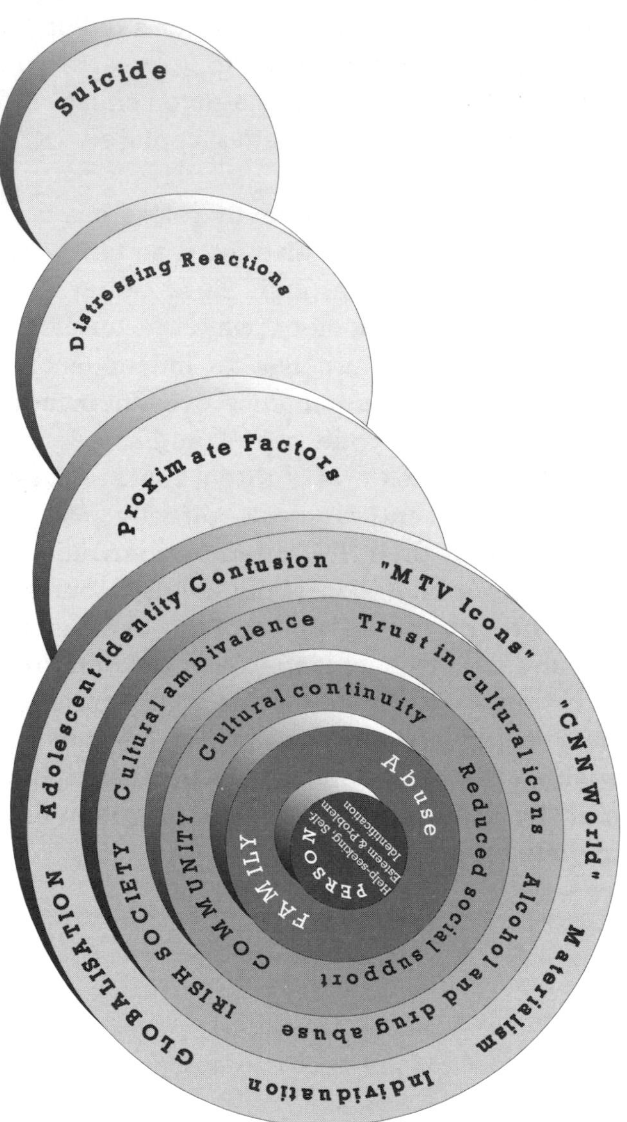

Figure 6.1: Schematic of Factors Leading to Suicide

Globalisation

The cultural codes of Irish society are increasingly influenced by a range of forces that impinge on us from outside our geographic boundaries, however defined. Such forces have of course always existed, but their increasing pervasiveness has come to constitute what has been described as "global culture", or *globalisation*.

> Globalisation is restructuring the way in which we live, and in a very profound manner. It is led from the West, bears the strong imprint of American political and economic power, and is highly uneven in its consequences (Giddens, 1999, p. 4).

Giddens goes on to say that we "must find ways to bring our runaway world to heel" (p. 5). While there are many facets to globalisation (technological, cultural, political, economic), some of which may be quite positive, there are also many victims, especially of economic globalisation, and especially in the poorer "developing" countries of the world (MacLachlan, 2003b).

It is undeniable that in many respects Ireland has been a beneficiary of globalisation. Offering both an English-speaking gateway to Europe and a well-educated workforce, the Celtic Tiger owes much to the massive economic investment from corporate North America. Indeed, today only 80 per cent of Ireland's export earnings are retained within our economy due to the involvement of multinationals (as reported in RTE's *Six One*, Friday, 31 January 2003). While emphasising that we recognise that North America is not the only globalising influence, and that such influence has benefited Ireland not only economically but culturally and indeed possibly politically too, it is important to recognise some of the possibly less desirable changes that are part of its "baggage".

A greater emphasis on the individual rather than the family or community; on material achievement, and on what you do rather than who you are; on pop and movie idols and on being like them if you want to be "cool", are just some of the social ramifications of globalisation in Ireland. The "CNN World" we now live in stacks up major events from across the globe for sound-biting entertainment in punchy newscasts, which despite their rapidity, continue throughout the day. Our world is a busy dramatic place — *you* should be busy and dramatic and exciting; that is, if you *wannabe* part of it. The inevitable downside of a focus on individual success is the consequences of individual failure, now with less diffusion of responsibility, the stakes are higher and with weakened community structures (church, Garda stations, post offices, bank branches and bus routes) there may be fewer people to share a burden with.

We live in an age when we are encouraged to believe that we *all* have some wonderful potential within us, *if only* we could discover what it is. And to not try and discover it can be almost as stigmatising as it is demoralising to find out that in your case, it is not actually true. Global culture also seems to transmit adolescent identity confusion, blurring the boundaries between childhood and adolescence on the one hand and between adolescence and adulthood on the other — the sense of transition, change and uncertainty seeming to start earlier and continuing longer. With this blurring comes a certain pressure to behave in a more mature, often sexualised manner (Britney Spears, Christina Aguilera, *N SYNC etc.) that holds the potential to be an additional stressor at this stage of development. As we reviewed in Chapter 5, for young men in particular, the meaning and value of being a man is in flux. The assuredness offered to them by traditional gender roles is quite, although not completely, elusive as both gender and sex are rethought and re-engineered. However — and this is a crucial point for appreciating the Irish situation — the effects of any particular facet of globalisation might well have been quite minimal if it were not for the sociocultural quagmire in which we now find ourselves. Culturally, we were ripe for the picking; for infusing with new values.

Culture and Community

Just as the English described syphilis as the "French disease" and the French described it as the "Italian disease", it is important not to fall into the trap of externalising the cause of our woes. Indeed, any sober analysis of Ireland's internal "state of mind" could hardly fail to identify our self-generated problems. For all of us, but especially for young people, recent years have witnessed a huge loss of trust in those who have traditionally been our "cultural icons". We have lost faith not only in individuals, but more fundamentally in the very institutions that sustained them. Priests, teachers, doctors, politicians, police, the judiciary and others have disappointed us; indeed, more than that: they have dismantled our feelings of identity with a coherent way of making a meaning out of life. In the gaps that this has opened up, values associated with globalisation now swirl and flow.

Also freely flowing, it would seem, is our consumption of alcohol and drugs. Now, wealthy as we are, we are all the better positioned to do to excess just about everything. With increasing liberalism, government reluctance to restrict alcohol use and corporate delight at its magnitude, Irish alcohol consumption has rocketed. As both a means of demonstrating one's strength while at the same time being seen as a (short-term) solution to problems arising as a result of perceived lack of strength, alcohol has lubricated many problems. The culture of conviviality that once imbued Irish pubs is being replaced by a more frenetic, almost chaotic and certainly public self-destruction. While we have acknowledged that alcohol may not be "the cause" of suicide it is surely clear that it puts many in "harm's way", both through its short-term dis-inhibiting effects and the longer-term belittling effects of its excessive use.

Alcohol consumption is a case in point where the traditions of a culture become increasingly maladaptive as the socio-economic context of that culture improves. Values that were once harmful but tolerable because of our relative poverty are increasingly harmful and increasingly intolerable. Yet the *auld* Ireland of the mighty *craic* down the pub is an image we are reluctant to shake off, as it is part of who we are — our cultural identity. As outlined in Chapter 2, most of us probably want to integrate the best of both the "old" and the "new" Irelands, and in many ways this *should* be the healthiest choice. Yet sometimes there are incompatible elements within these two domains. Others long for the "old" Ireland and feel, at a very personal level, the negative consequences of its decline without experiencing the benefits of the rising "new" Ireland; thus, the culture in which this group exist is not the one with which they identify and the culture with which they identify is fading at what must seem, to them, an alarming rate.

Our own preliminary research (Smyth and MacLachlan, 2002) suggests that it is those who are most ambivalent — who are not particularly for or against either the "old" or the "new" — who may be most at risk because, perhaps not knowing what they want or how they feel about their own culture, they are ironically left wanting in terms of some stabilising identity. In Chapter 4 we also reviewed how the loss of cultural continuity removed a potential anchor for those seeking personal continuity during adolescence when the self often develops through redefinition. Without meaningful "terms of cultural reference", this task becomes more challenging and possibly more disorienting. The angst and terror that a strong cultural identity can put at bay (see Chapter 3) may, in the absence of that identity, rise increasingly close to the surface and give way to thoughts about the meaning of life, one's place in it and the possibility of escaping from something with which you cannot identify.

Family and Self

Without doubt, one of the greatest crises in Irish family life has been the realisation of the extent of child abuse. Once again, we have "externalised" much of this by focusing, in particular, on clerical child abuse. Sadly, clerical abuse is only the most visible tip of the child abuse which has and continues to take place, where most cases occur in the family (Lawlor, 2002). Indeed in Ireland, sexual abuse perpetrated by clerics is far less frequent (1.9 per cent in the case of men and 1.4 per cent in the case of women) than abuse at the hands of family members or individuals who are non-family members but who are known to the child (McGee et al., 2002). This, like suicide, is another taboo topic in Ireland which we fail to address at our peril — at our children's peril.

In Chapter 4, we reviewed Stillion and McDowell's (1996) Suicide Trajectory Model, which lists various familial factors that might be implicated in suicides. These included early experiences of loss, parental conflict and parental suicidal behaviour. However, it is also important to emphasise the tremendous good that families do in supporting suicidal members and perhaps preventing suicides without even being aware that such drastic action was ever considered. Equally, there will be some circumstances when no matter how supportive or loving family members are, an individual decides to take their own life. In such cases, there may simply have been nothing *anyone* could have done to prevent it. In these circumstances, it is important that our focus on familial factors not be turned into a situation where blame is apportioned to the friends or family of the deceased.

Various models of suicidal behaviour identify individual risk factors that may be related to suicide. For instance, Jenkins and Singh's pyramidal model places suicide at the top of a pyramid with "Use of means of suicide", "Access to means", "Suicide Ideation", "Depressive Thoughts", "Factors Causing Depression" (such as negative events in one's life, chronic socially stressful situations, and a lack of social support from others) all underpinning suicide at progressively lower and broader levels of the pyramid. In Figure 6.1, we refer to such "Factors Causing Depression" as "Proximate Factors", which may lead to a variety of "Distressing Reactions" and, for some, to "Suicide". The way in which such proximate factors, distressing reactions and suicide itself are in turn responded to is also, we have argued, a cultural and societal matter. However, the model presented in Figure 6.1 is primarily concerned with detailing the "ultimate" socio-cultural factors that we believe direct, particularly young males in Irish society, along suicidal pathways.

While a two-tier health system, poorly developed primary care services, poorly integrated acute and community care services and a strongly medically oriented mental health service are problematic for responding to the needs of those contemplating suicide, our primary concern in this chapter is to consider factors related to prevention.

Shifting the Focus

Throughout, we have made reference to the limitations of the traditional psychological and psychiatric/medical conceptions of suicide and suicide prevention. Here we briefly outline the merits of an Action Theory perspective (Michel and Valach,

2001), as it may be applied to suicide. In general terms, actions are said to be associated with both cognitive and emotional processes which involve planning, monitoring and decision-making, with an individual's actions relating to their views of the self, career goals and broader life plans. Both internal and external elements (including social and cultural settings, exposure and experiences) are considered. In short, *people think through what they are doing*:

> actions are the result of conscious, unconscious and semi-conscious, goal-directed, planned and intended processes, which are cognitively and socially steered, controlled and regulated (Michel and Valach, 2001, p. 235).

This is not to suggest that their thinking is necessarily clear, accurate or justified, or indeed that their resulting acts are to be considered reasonable, but more that they are nonetheless *reasoned* and not simply random acts of madness.

Michel and Valach (2001) go on to delineate three consequences of viewing suicide and its prevention in this manner. First, the relationship between helper and helped must differ in fundamental ways from the traditional framework. The helper must recognise that the individual is indeed an expert in their own actions and thus should be afforded equal status and level of power in the therapeutic relationship. Second, it must be understood that an individual's suicidal behaviour is embedded in the context of the rest of their lives and, as such, ought not to be seen as an isolated expression of pathology, to be understood mechanistically and as something to be "fixed". Suicidal behaviour may therefore be seen as a goal-directed action in its own right — a possible solution (albeit transient and undesirable) to the unbearable situation being experienced by the individual. Finally, and paradoxically, this perspective views suicide as an act of "self-preservation". Here "self" is seen as the essence of being rather than the physical reality of existence. A person's distress may be so severe that the "out" which suicide offers may be the only way (in their eyes) to preserve their self-concept, identity and perhaps even their dignity.

Unlike other hospital admissions, people entering the health system as a result of some form of suicidal behaviour are not there as a result of some illness which befell them, but more often as a result of conscious, planned and self-directed action. Thus, an alternative, more contextual and inclusive perspective is required. We need to move away from seeing prevention as the sole concern of healthcare professionals (the "experts") who have to "fix" the "glitch" in the "system" of the "patient" who behaved "pathologically". As such, focus is shifted away from the "professional-as-expert" perspective that many suicidal individuals report as unhelpful and off-putting and which only adds to their sense of isolation and of feeling misunderstood (Isometsa et al., 1995).

While clearly the expertise of mental health practitioners is a valuable resource with regard to suicide, there is also the danger that "over-professionalising" it may scare off initiatives that ordinary people may take to prevent suicide. If one accepts the importance of a cultural perspective and the value of community interventions for suicide, one must also accept that those without formal training in mental health may well be at the vanguard of change. Indeed, a society that is content to simply "refer" potentially suicidal people to specialists is one that fails to locate the problem in itself. In this scenario, the "shrink" simply legitimises the feelings of social exclusion that may drive individuals to further diminish and, perhaps, even kill themselves. The site for prevention of suicide must be "ordinary life", not "life in crises", when one is least able to take on board what one most needs to know.

Identifying Youth at Risk

A great difficulty regarding suicide prevention is the inability of the systems already in place to identify those who are at risk of making a suicide attempt. In the case of clinical depression (a recognised risk for suicidal behaviour), it is not the diagnosis itself, but obviously the "owner" of that diagnosis who may initiate suicidal behaviour (thus making suicide both individual and idiosyncratic). Isometsa et al. (1995) go on to report that at least 50 per cent of those who go on to die by suicide have visited a physician in the month prior to death; however, suicide is discussed in only a minority of these visits. The number of cases in which suicide was addressed ranged from 39 per cent in the case of psychiatric outpatient visits and 11 per cent in general-practice visits to 6 per cent of those who visited other medical specialists. Clearly, there is a problem with communication here both in the identification of risk and discussion surrounding it, which likely acts as one of the key barriers to the identification of risk and the prevention of suicide.

In addition to difficulties concerning the communication of suicide ideation, traditional biomedical and psychological models often adopt a causal and linear model when considering suicide. Bancroft et al. (1979) identified clear incongruencies between healthcare professionals and suicidal individuals in the *type* of thinking surrounding suicide. The former were reported to think in terms of the *causes* of suicide while the latter speak of suicide in terms of the *reasons* or *motives* behind the behaviour. This difference is central, as Hinkle and Schmidt (as cited by Michel et al., 2001) summarise: *reasons* offer an explanation in terms of the preceding intentions behind the action, while *causes* explain an action in terms of the properties of the environment that resulted in the action or made the action occur. This is a clear distinction and one which people are capable of making in everyday circumstances (Michel, Valach and Waeber, 1994).

In order to approach the issue of suicide prevention, we first must see suicide as preventable and suicide prevention as acceptable and desirable. This specific point is addressed in a comprehensive review of the area by Miller et al. (1999). These authors argue that suicide intervention/prevention *has* to be seen as an *extension* of healthcare provision for the youth population. This is in keeping with recommendations from others in the area such as Dryfoos (1994) and Gutkin (1995) where suicide prevention is not considered to be a specialist-oriented or isolated aspect of healthcare. This perspective marks an important move away from seeing suicide as a problem for psychiatric or mental health settings alone and recognises the important role schools and educators can play in issues of adolescent mental health generally, and suicide prevention more specifically. Furthermore, these authors suggest that few studies have been done of the acceptability of approaches to suicide prevention. This paucity of knowledge in the area appears to be a rather obvious omission, as the likelihood of a programme being implemented is fundamentally tied to the way in which it is "sold" to schools, its level of acceptability and the degree of comfort programme presenters feel with the material. This observation importantly positions schools as consumers of psychological, sociological and cultural information and interventions.

The aforementioned study (Miller et al., 1999) examined the three most common types of suicide prevention programme: (1) curriculum-based presentations to students; (2) in-service training for teachers; and (3) student self-report, school-wide screening for identification of at-risk individuals. The principal aims of such programmes are (a) to heighten awareness among students regarding suicide; (b) to train students to recognise possible signs of suicidal behaviour in order to assist others and better understand the experience; and (c) to provide students with information on available school and community-based sources of help (Shaffer et al., 1988). The noted outcomes of suicide prevention programmes include effective change in students' knowledge and attitudes towards suicide, a positive influence on previously unidentified suicidal adolescents and an increase in the likelihood of adolescents disclosing to parents/adults information on peers who are at risk. When the level of acceptability of each of the three programmes was assessed, it was found that the school-wide screening of students for the identification of at-risk cases was *least* acceptable among both parents and educators. Suggested explanations for this finding included a feeling that adequate services do not exist to deal with such information, that the "labelling" of students in this manner may serve to increase an individual's isolation and stigmatisation and may worsen the problem it seeks to address. In spite of this, the screening method of suicide prevention remains common and is thoroughly in keeping with the biomedical approach, with some even suggesting that such screening is a vital part of *any* prevention package (Miller and DuPaul, 1996; Reynolds and Mazza, 1994).

Moving to consider the other two approaches (provision of information to students and in-service training to teachers), these were seen to be equally acceptable and were generally viewed in favourable terms and, as such, are more likely to be implemented in a school setting. In addition, the high level of acceptability of these two approaches suggests that educators recognise the need for a two-strand approach whereby *both* teachers and students are involved in the prevention process.

Despite these positive findings, there remains concern in some quarters that the very mention of suicide (perhaps most especially in the form of suicide prevention programmes) motivates people to behave in a suicidal manner. It is of fundamental importance to note that this is something which has been extensively investigated, with the Centers for Disease Control (in the United States) reaching the clear conclusion that ". . . there is absolutely no evidence for this . . ."(Centers for Disease Control, 1992). Kalafat and Elias (1995) assert, on this basis, that the widespread implementation of school-based prevention programmes is a must in our approach to suicide prevention. Although the statistics indicate that more completed suicides take place in the 20–24 year old bracket, a more proactive approach is required whereby younger people are targeted for support *before* the point of highest risk occurs. Furthermore, and from a practical perspective, adolescents within the school system are relatively easily involved in such programmes, more easily than at older ages when gathering groups together presents more obstacles to both programme research and implementation. With specific regard to the type of information included in such prevention programmes, Kalafat et al. (1995) assert that programmes must *supplement* rather than replace existing healthcare education. This reflects the long-standing, public-health approach to mental health of Caplan (1964) which states that in "the absence of a knowledge of the causes of mental disorders, primary prevention must be directed toward improving non-specific helping resources in the community" (p. 30). Such thinking blends well with our own culture-based approach.

Given that educational programmes of the kind discussed here are most likely not adolescents' first encounter with suicide (indeed, over 75 per cent of adolescents report previous exposure to the issue of suicide, either at a personal or abstract level (Kalafat and Elias, 1992)), Kalafat et al. (1995) go on to make some specific recommendations which may be summarised as follows:

- Programmes are to have a practical, educational rather than clinical focus.
- While curriculum additions are certainly to be welcomed, a stand-alone approach is unlikely to be effective, thus marking the need for a broad-spectrum, proactive, community-wide approach.
- Material must be problem-centred rather than content-centred, thus adding a clearly practical component which fits well within the school setting.
- School staff must be viewed by students (or come to be viewed by students) as approachable outside of their formal roles. The authors note that this is one of the more difficult aspects to implement as it, perhaps above and beyond others, calls for additional resources. Nonetheless, it is a vital component in the holistic support and education of adolescents.
- Administrative policies and procedures for responding to at-risk students, students who have attempted to end their own life or in the aftermath of a completed suicide must be put in place. This may involve the development and training of school-based crisis response teams.
- Educational programmes for all adults involved in or in contact with the school system. These should address warning signs, initial response, referral and available resources/ sources of help.
- Classroom educational programmes for students covering risk/warning signs, initial response, the process of referral and those resources that are available in their own school setting.
- Ensuring that there are established and known links between schools and wider community-based carers/healthcare professionals. This way, the intervention/prevention crosses over between school and community life.

- Development of clear and supportive procedures for the return of a student who has made a suicide attempt to the school system. This can also include the practical component of the school being informed of the student's return.

This perspective stresses the value of a multi-agency response to mental health generally (including suicide) where the "community" of school is involved in every stage of caring for the adolescent's development, ranging from academic/scholastic achievement to general health and well-being and emotional support. This latter point is especially important when we recognise that, historically, the family has been given primary responsibility for these aspects of childcare and development. While this approach at least had some chance of success within the confines of the traditional nuclear family, the many and varied family structures of today mean that, in some cases, sole care for the adolescent's well-being cannot securely rest within the family and that perhaps, a broadening of the definition itself may be called for. As such, the inclusion of the school and broader community in which the adolescent exists and develops is clearly warranted and to be approached with optimism for prevention opportunity rather than the unfounded reluctance which currently exists.

Having highlighted how schools could contribute to suicide prevention, it would be remiss indeed not to mention how the culture of our schooling system, and particularly the huge emphasis on academic achievement, may be a contributory factor to mental health problems. "Academic achievement first, then life after" seems to be the motto not only of many of our schools, but also of the ambitious parents who send them there, and, as a result, "an education for life" is often overlooked. Students seem to be increasingly focused on the end-product of "points", not only at secondary and tertiary level, but also now at the primary level where "grinds" are edging their way in. Some of our own research indicates that perceived poor school performance is the primary stressor for many of our children. Clearly, if the sort of prevention programmes we are referring to are to be included in students' school time, something else will have to be taken out. Are we, as a society, as schools, as parents and as students, prepared to put our health, our relationships and our compassion above academic achievement, if even for only an hour a week?

If not, then we are indeed cultivating many problems, including suicide.

Another issue which we must address is the role the media can play with regard to the presentation of information on suicide. While we are *not* proposing that Ireland's media take over the role of parenting our youth, the ways in which programmes like *Exploring Masculinities* (discussed in Chapter 5) and suicide itself are represented and discussed have a considerable and significant influence on our collective understanding and appreciation of the suicide phenomenon. Headlines such as "Masculinity under threat from new school programme",[1] "Boys taught to be violent",[2] "Soft Porn and Soggy Poetry",[3] "When men are made ashamed",[4] and "Male Suicide and Feminism"[5] misrepresent the actual state of Irish youth suicide research and prevention initiatives and mislead public opinion. The media generally has a responsibility to cultivate a more informed and empathetic culture. In this, they often fail, with headlines such as those above merely illustrating the easier and more sensationalist way in which to approach this topical issue.

CONCLUSIONS

Carr (2003) argues that, in the case of the rapid increase in male suicides among indigenous communities of the South Pacific (including Australia and New Zealand), the salient factors "reflect forms of alienation from the wider community" (p. 373). The quote from Eckersley at the head of this chapter also suggests that "the cultural focus on the individual 'self' has weakened social cohesion, undermined the sense of belonging, and left the

---

[1] Letter from Mary T. Cleary of AMEN to *Irish Independent*, 21 September 2000.

[2] Feature piece as part of "Men in Crisis" series, by Ian O'Doherty in the *Evening Herald*, 28 September 2000.

[3] Opinion column by Brendan Glacken, *Irish Times* 15 March 2001.

[4] Opinion column by John Waters, *Irish Times*, 22 October 2001.

[5] Letter by Phil Mac Ghiolla of AMEN to *Irish Times*, 22 November 2001.

self dangerously exposed and isolated . . .". Together, these quotes suggest a mixture of processes related to self-focus on the one hand and exclusion from others on the other hand. MacLachlan (2003b) has argued that existentially, each of us needs to have the feeling of *being somebody in a world that matters*, and that often if migrant groups lose this identity, then their mental health suffers. In Ireland, we are all participants — willing or not — in a temporal cultural migration, from the idea of a traditional Ireland to the experience of contemporary Ireland.

We cannot fudge the fundamental questions of our existence or how that existence has changed. Equally, we cannot pretend that these are not important concerns for our young and emerging adults to contemplate. Our government's default policy of fumbling through cultural change exemplifies the directionless confusion that many young people experience in trying to establish just *who they are* and just *what does matter*. Our aim should not, of course, be to provide simplistic answers to such questions, but rather to make discussion of these issues, and recognition of the angst that may accompany them, appropriate topics of discussion and exploration *in places that matter* — our schools.

The Department of Education's handling of the *Exploring Masculinities* programme is nothing short of a disgrace and clearly illustrates the general approach to topics such as youth suicide. Surely if a topic is important enough to justify the development of a specific programme, then it is also important enough to require its implementation, assessment and public discussion of that assessment. If it doesn't "work", then let's fix it.

The way in which we as a society create meaning of the world we now live in is perhaps not that different from the challenge that has perennially faced adolescents through the ages. If we are to save some individuals from the tragedy of their own suicidal despair, it will be through their *explicit* inclusion in a process that recognises the difficulties they and many others face. Such an initiative should not be a "confessional" of weakness or inadequacy, but rather a means for thinking through what matters in life and what to do when you feel that life doesn't matter any more. Cultural transition, self-identity, alcohol and drug use, suicide and child abuse, are but *some* of the problems that will not go away by *not* talking about them, or pretending that they are not a key aspect of the lives of our school children. Such issues deserve the same space and attention in our school system that they demand in the lives of our children.

We hope that our alternative view is a first step towards asking those questions that have not previously been asked in an Irish context and applying to our own situation what has been learned elsewhere with regard to the way in which culture and society creates and shapes our understanding of the world around us and the way we function within it.

References

Allen, W.R. and Farley, R. (1986), "The shifting social and economic tides of Black America", *Annual Review of Sociology*, 12, 277-306.

Alvarez, A. (1971), *The Savage God*, New York: Random House.

Amit-Talai, V. (1995), "Conclusion: The 'multi' cultural of youth", in V. Amit-Talai and H. Wulff (eds.), *Youth Cultures: A cross-Cultural Perspective*, London: Routledge.

Anthony, S. (1971), *The Discovery of Death in Childhood and After*, Harmondsworth: Allen Lane.

Aquinas, St. T. (1929), *Summa Theologica*, London: Burns, Oates and Washbourne.

Aries, P. (1960), *Centuries of Childhood: A Social History of Family Life*, Baldick, R. (trans.), New York: Knoff.

Arnett, J. (1991), "Adolescents and Heavy Metal Music: From the Mouths of the Metalheads", *Youth and Society*, 23, 76-98.

Arnett, J. (1999), "Adolescent Storm and Stress, Reconsidered", *American Psychologist*, 54(7), 317-326.

Bancroft, J., Hawton, K., Simkin, S., Kingston, B., Cumming, C. and Whitwell, D. (1979), "The reasons people give for taking overdoses: a further inquiry", *British Journal of Medical Psychology*, 52, 353-365.

Barber, J.G. (2001), "Relative misery and youth suicide", *Australian and New Zealand Journal of Psychiatry*, 35(1), 49-57.

Beautrais, A.L. (2000), "Methods of youth suicide in New Zealand: trends and implications for prevention", *The Australian and New Zealand Journal of Psychiatry*, 34(3), 413-419.

Beautrais, A.L., Joyce, P.R. and Mulder, R.T. (1997), "Precipitating Factors and Life Events in Serious Suicide Attempts Among Youths Aged 13 Through 24 Years", *American Academy of Child and Adolescent Psychiatry*, 36(11), 1543-1551.

Beck, A.T. (1963), "Thinking and Depression", *Archives of General Psychiatry*, 1, 324-333.

Beck, A.T. (1967), *Depression: Clinical, Experimental and Theoretical Aspects*, New York: Hoebner Medical Division, Harper & Row.

Becker, E. (1968), *The Structure of Evil: An Essay on the Unification of the Science of Man*, New York: Braziller.

Becker, E. (1971), *The Birth and Death of Meaning (2nd Ed.)*, New York: The Free Press.

Becker, E. (1973), *The Denial of Death*, New York: Free Press.

Berenbaum, S.A. and Hines, M. (1992), "Early androgens are related to childhood sex-typed toy preferences" *Psychological Science*, 3, 203-206.

Berman, A.L. (1997), "The Adolescent: The Individual in Cultural Perspective", *Suicide and Life-Threatening Behaviour*, 27(1), 5-14.

Berry, J.W. (1969), *The Education of American Indians: A Survey of the Literature*, Washington, DC: US Government Printing Office (Document 24-230).

Berry, J.W. (1997), "Lead Article: Immigration, Acculturation and Adaptation", *Applied Psychology: An International Review*, 46, 5-68.

Berry, J.W. and Kim, U. (1988), "Acculturation and mental health" in P. Dasen, J.W. Berry and N. Sartorius (eds.), *Health and Cross-Cultural Psychology*, London: Sage.

Blumenthal, S.J. and Kupfer, D.J. (1988), "Overview of early detection and treatment strategies for suicidal behavior in young people", *Journal of Youth and Adolescence*, 17, 1-23.

Boergers, J., Spirito, A. and Donaldson, D. (1998), "Reasons for Adolescent Suicide Attempts: Associations With Psychological Functioning", *Journal of the American Academy of Child and Adolescent Psychiatry*, 37(12), 1287-1293.

Bowers, F. (1994), *Suicide in Ireland*, Dublin: Irish Medical Organisation.

Brent, D.A. and Moritz, G. (1993), *Gender, conduct disorder and suicide: An explanation of the gender differences in adolescent suicide*, Paper presented at the Rochester Symposium on Developmental Psychopathology, Rochester, NY, 5 October.

Bryson, B. (1996), "'Anything but heavy metal': Symbolic exclusion and musical dislikes", *American Sociological Review*, 61, 884-899.

Canetto, S.S. (1997a), "Gender and suicidal behaviour: Theories and evidence", in R. Maris, A. Silverman and S.S. Canetto (eds.), *Review of Suicidology*, New York: Guilford Press.

Canetto, S.S. (1997b), "Meanings of Gender and Suicidal Behaviour during Adolescence", *Suicide and Life-Threatening Behaviour*, 27(4), 339-351.

Caplan, G. (1964), *Principles of Preventative Psychiatry*, New York: Basic Books.

Carr, S.C. (2003), *Social Psychology: Context, Communication and Culture*, Sydney: John Wiley & Sons.

Centers for Disease Control (1992), *Youth Suicide Prevention Programs: A Resource Guide*, Atlanta: Centers for Disease Control.

Chandler, M.J. and Lalonde, C. (1998), "Cultural Continuity as a Hedge Against Suicide in Canada's First Nations", *Transcultural Psychiatry*, 35(2), 191-219.

Clare, A. (2000), *On Men*, London: Arrow Books.

Cole, D. (1989), "Psychopathology of adolescent suicide: Hopelessness, coping beliefs and depression", *Journal of Abnormal Psychology*, 98, 248-255.

Coroner's Act, S.I.N. (1962 (FORMS) Regulations).

Coupe, N.M. (2000), "The epidemiology of Maori suicide in Aotearoa/ New Zealand" in F.H. Bolitho, S.C. Carr and B.M. O'Reilly (eds.), *Psychology in the South Pacific: Global, Local and Glocal Applications*, New Zealand: Massey University (http://spjp.massey.ac.nz.books/bolitho/contents.shtml).

Cuddy-Casey, M. and Orvaschel, H. (1997), "Children's understanding of death in relation to child suicidality and homicidality", *Clinical Psychology Review*, 17(1), 33-46.

Curran, D.K. (1987), *Adolescent Suicidal Behaviour*, New York: Hemisphere.

De Wilde, E.J. (2000), Adolescent Suicidal Behaviour: A General Population Perspective, in K. Hawton and K. Van Heeringen (eds.), *The International Handbook of Suicide and Attempted Suicide*, Chichester: John Wiley and Sons.

Demos, J. (1986), *Past, Present and Personal: The Family and the Life Course in American History*, New York: Oxford University Press.

Department of Education (1997), *Balance: Who Cares?* Dublin: The Equality Committee, Department of Education.

Department of Education and Science (2000), *Exploring Masculinities*, Dublin: Government Publications.

Department of Health and Children (2002), *Strategic Task Force on Alcohol Interim Report*, Dublin: Government Publications.

Diekstra, R.F.W. (1994), *On the Burden of Suicide*, Cork: O'Leary Ltd.

Dinneen, P.S. (1927), *Focloir Gaedhilge agus Bearla, An Irish-English Dictionary*, Dublin, Cork.

Dizmang, L., Watson, J., May, P. and Bopp, J. (1974), "Adolescent suicide at the Indian reservation", *American Journal of Orthopsychiatry*, 44, 43-49.

Dominian, J. (1990), *Depression*, Glasgow: WM Collins and Sons.

Dryfoos, J.G. (1994), *Full-service schools: A Revolution in Health and Social Services for Children, Youth and Families*, San Francisco, CA: Jossey-Bass.

Dubow, E.F., Kausch, D.F., Blum, M.C., Reed, J. and Bush, E. (1989), "Correlates of suicidal ideation and attempts in a community sample of junior high and high school students", *Journal of Clinical Child Psychology*, 18, 158-166.

Durkheim, E. (1897/1951), *Suicide: A Study of Sociology*, J.A. Spaulding and C. Simpson (trans.), London: Routledge and Kegan Paul. (Original work published 1897.)

Early, K.E. and Askers, R.L. (1993), "It's a White thing": An Exploration of Beliefs about Suicide in the African American Community, *Deviant Behaviour*, 14, 227-296.

EchoHawk, M. (1997), "Suicide: The Scourge of the Native American People", *Suicide and Life-Threatening Behaviour*, 27(1), 60-67.

Eckersley, R. (1997), "Psychological disorders in young people: On the agenda but not the mend", *Medical Journal of Australia*, 166, 423-424.

Ehrhardt, A.A., Meyer-Bahlburg, H.F., Rosen, L.R., Feldman, J.F., Veridiano, N.P., Elkin, E.J. and McEwan, B.S. (1989), "The development of gender-related behaviour in females following prenatal exposure to diethylbestrol (DES)", *Hormones and Behaviour*, 23(4), 526-541.

Ellis, J.B. and Range, L. (1988), "Femininity and reasons for living", *Educational and Psychological Research*, 8, 9-24.

Ferree, M.M., Lorber, J. and Hess, B.B. (1999), *Revisioning Gender*, London: Sage Publications.

Freud, A. (1958), "Adolescence", *Psychoanalytic Study of the Child*, 15, 255-278.

Freud, A. (1968), "Adolescence" in A.E. Winder and D. Angus (eds.), *Adolescence: Contemporary Studies*, New York: American Books.

Freud, A. (1969), "Adolescence as a developmental disturbance" in G. Caplan and S. Lebovici (eds.), *Adolescence: Psychosocial Perspectives*, New York: Basic Books.

Gaines, D. (1991), *Teenage Wasteland*, New York: Pantheon.

Garrison, C.Z., Addy, C.L., Kirby, L.J., McKeown, R.E. and Waller, J.L. (1991), "A longitudinal study of suicidal ideation in young adolescents", *Journal of the American Academy of Child and Adolescent Psychiatry*, 30, 597-603.

Gergen, K. and Gergen, M. (1996), *Toward a Cultural Constructionist Psychology*, Retrieved 29 January 2002, from Swathmore University, http://www.swathmore.edu/SocSci/kgergen1/tccp.html.

Gibbs, J.T. (1988), "Conceptual, methodological and sociocultural issues in Black youth suicide: Implications for assessment and early intervention", *Suicide and Life-Threatening Behaviour*, 18, 73-89.

Giddens, A. (1991), *Modernity and Self Identity*, Stanford, CA: Stanford University Press.

Giddens, A. (1999), *Runaway World: How Globalisation is Reshaping Our Lives*, London: Profile Books.

Gleeson, J. (1999), *Exploring Masculinities External Evaluation Executive Summary*, University of Limerick: Department of Education and Professional Studies.

Goldney, R.D. (2001), "The media and suicide: A cautionary view" *Crisis*, 22(4), 173-175.

Grullman, E.A. (1971), *Suicide: Prevention, Intervention, Postvention*, Boston: Beacon Press.

Gutkin, T.B. (1995), "School psychology and health care: Moving service delivery into the twenty-first century", *School Psychology Quarterly*, 10, 236-246.

Haber, H. (1994), *Beyond Postmodern Politics*, New York: Routledge.

Habermas, J. (1991), "The paradigm shift in Mead", in M. Aboulafia (ed.), *Philosophy, Social Theory and the Thought of George Herbert Mead*, Albany: State University of New York Press.

Haim, A. (1974), *Adolescent Suicide*, New York: International University Press.

Handy, C. (1994), *The Empty Raincoat: Making Sense of the Future*, London: Random House.

Harré, R. (1979), *Social Being: A Theory for Social Psychology*, Oxford: Blackwell.

Harry, J. (1983), "Parasuicide, gender and gender deviance", *Journal of Health and Social Behviour*, 24, 350-361.

Hawton, K. (1999), "Effects of a drug-overdose in a television drama on presentations to hospital for self-poisoning: Time series and questionnaire study", *British Medical Journal*, 318, 972-977.

Hawton, K., Cole, D.A., O'Grady, J. and Osborn, M. (1982), "Motivational aspects of deloberage self-poisoning in adolescents" *British Journal of Psychiatry*, 141, 286-291.

Hawton, K., Fagg, J., Simkin, S., Harriss, L. and Malmberg, A. (1998), "Methods used for suicide by farmers in England and Wales — The contribution of availability and its relevance to prevention" *British Journal of Psychiatry*, 173, 320-324.

Hermans, H.J.M. and Kempen, H.J.G. (1998), "Moving Cultures: The Perilous Problems of Cultural Dichotomies in a Globalizing Society", *American Psychologist*, 53(10), 1111-1120.

Hibell, B., Andersson, B., Ahlstrom, S., Balakireva, O., Bjarnasson, T., Kokkevi, A. and Morgan, M. (2000), *The 1999 ESPAD Report: Alcohol and Other Drug Use Among Students in 30 European Countries*, The Swedish Council for Information on Alcohol and Other Drugs, The Pompidou Group at the Council of Europe.

Hovey, J. and King, C.A. (1996), "Acculturative Stress, Depression and Suicidal Ideation among Immigrant and Second-Generation Latino Adolescents", *Journal of the American Academy of Child and Adolescent Psychiatry*, 35(9), 1183-1192.

Hume, D. (1783/1929), *An Essay on Suicide*, Yellow Springs, OH: Kahoe.

Iga, M. (1986), *The Thorn in the Chrysanthemum*, Berkley: University of California Press.

Inglehart, R. and Baker, W.E. (2000), "Modernization, cultural change and the persistence of traditional values", *American Sociological Review*, 65(1), 19-51.

Irish Association of Suicidology (2000a), *Media Guidelines on the Portrayal of Suicide*, Mayo: Connaught Telegraph.

Irish Association of Suicidology (2000b), *Proceedings of the Fifth Annual Conference: Youth Suicide*, Mayo: Connaught Telegraph.

Irish Association of Suicidology and National Suicide Review Group (2002), *Suicide Prevention in Schools: Best Practice Guidelines*, Mayo: Connaught Telegraph.

Isometsa, E.T., Henriksson, M., Marttunen, M., Heikkinen, H.M., Aro, H., Kuoppasalmi, K. and Lonquvist, J.K. (1995), "Mental disorders in young and midd*le-aged men who commit suicide" British Medical Journal, 310*, 1366-1367.

James, S., Hartnett, S.A. and Kalsbeek, W.D. (1983), "John Henryism and blood pressure differences among black men", *Journal of Behavioural Medicine*, 6, 259-278.

Janssen, J., Dechesne, M. and van Knippenberg, A. (1999), "The Psychological Importance of Youth Culture", *Youth and Society*, 31(2), 152-167.

Jenkins, R. and Singh, B. (2000), "General Population Strategies of Suicide Prevention" in K. Hawton and K. Van Heeringen (eds.), *International Handbook of Suicide and Attempted Suicide*, Chichester: John Wiley and Sons.

Jobes, D.A., Berman, A.L., O'Carroll, P., Eastgard, S. and Knickmwyer, S. (1996), "The Kurt Cobain suicide crisis: Perspectives from research, public health and the news media", *Suicide and Life-Threatening Behaviour*, 26(3), 260-271.

Kalafat, J. and Elias, M.J. (1992), "Adolescents' experience with and response to suicidal peers", *Suicide and Life-Threatening Behaviour*, 22, 315-321.

Kalafat, J. and Elias, M.J. (1995), "Suicide prevention in an educational context: Broad and narrow foci", *Suicide and Life-Threatening Behaviour*, 25(1), 123-136.

Kane, B. (1979), "Children's concepts of death", *The Journal of Genetic Psychology*, 134, 141-153.

Kastenbaum, R.J. (2001), *Death, Society and Human Experience* (7th Ed.), Boston: Allyn and Bacon.

Kazarian, S.S. and Persad, E. (2001), "Cultural Issues in Suicidal Behaviour", in S.S. Kazarian and D.R. Evans (eds.), *Handbook of Cultural Health Psychology*, London: Academic Press.

Kelleher, M.J. (1996), *Suicide and the Irish*, Cork: Mercier Press.

Kelleher, M.J. (1998), "Youth suicide trends in the Republic of Ireland", *British Journal of Psychiatry*, 173, 196-197.

Kelleher, M.J., Corcoran, P., Keeley, H.S., Dennehy, J. and O'Donnell, I. (1996), "Improving Procedures for Recording Suicide Statistics", *Irish Medical Journal*, 89(1), 14-15.

Kelleher, M.J., Keeley, H.S., Chambers, D. and Corcoran, P. (2000), "Suicide" in F. Henn, N. Sartorius, H. Helmchen and H. Lauter (eds.), *Contemporary Psychiatry*, Heidelberg: Springer GmbH.

Kelly, F. (1988), *A Guide to Early Irish Law*, Dublin: Dublin Institute for Advanced Studies.

Kenny, C. (2001), *Suicidal Children and Adolescents*, Wiltshire: The Cromwell Press.

King, S.R., Hampton, W.R., Bernstein, B. and Schichor, A. (1996), "College students' views on suicide", *Journal of American College Health*, 44(6), 283-287.

Klein, N. (2000), *No Logo*, London: Flamingo.

Kosky, R.J., Eshkevari, H.S., Goldney, R. and Hassan, R. (1998), *Suicide Prevention: The Global Context*, New York: Kluwer Academic.

Kraemer, S. (2000), "The Fragile Male", *British Medical Journal*, 321, 1609-1612.

Kumar, G. and Steer, R.A. (1995), "Psychosocial correlates of suicidal ideation in adolescent psychiatric inpatients", *Suicide and Life-Threatening Behaviour*, 25(3), 339-347.

Langford, R.A., Ritchie, J. and Ritchie, J. (1998), "Suicidal Behaviour in a Bicultural Society: A Review of Gender and Cultural Differences in Adolescents and Young Personal of Aotearoa/New Zealand" *Suicide and Life-Threatening Behaviour*, 28(1), 94-105.

Lawlor, K. (2002), *Child Sexual Abuse in Sub-Saharan Africa*, Paper presented at the Department of Psychology, Trinity College Dublin Research Seminar 2001/2002.

Leonard, E.C. (2001), "Confidential Death to Prevent Suicidal Contagion: An Accepted But Never Implemented, Nineteenth-Century Idea", *Suicide and Life-Threatening Behaviour*, 31(4), 460-466.

Lesage, A.D., Boyer, R., Grunberg, F., Vanier, C., Morissette, R., Menard-Buteau, C. and Loyer, M. (1994), "Suicide and Mental Disorders: A Case-Control Study of Young Men", *American Journal of Psychiatry*, 151, 1063-1068.

Lester, D. and Whipple, M. (1996), "Music Preference, Depression, Suicidal Preoccupation and Personality: Comment on Stack and Grundlach's Papers", *Suicide and Life-Threatening Behaviour*, 26, 68-70.

Lewinsohn, P.M., Rohde, P. and Seeley, J.R. (1993), "Psychosocial characteristics of adolescents with a history of suicide attempt", *Journal of the American Academy of Child and Adolescent Psychiatry*, 32, 60-68.

Lewis, R.J. and Shepeard, G. (1992), "Inferred characteristics of successful suicides as function of gender and context" *Suicide and Life-Threatening Behaviour*, 22, 187-198.

Linehan, M.M. (1973), "Suicide and attempted suicide: Study of perceived sex differences", *Perceptual and Motor Skills*, 37, 31-34.

Lott, B. and Maluso, D. (1993), "The social learning of gender" in A.E. Beall and R.J. Sternberg (eds.), The Psychology of Gender, New York: Guilford Press.

Lourie, R.S. (1957), "Suicide and attempted suicide in children and adolescents" *Texas Medical Review* (as cited by Dominian, 1990), 58-68.

MacLachlan, M. (1997), *Culture and Health*, London: Wiley.

MacLachlan, M. and O'Connell, M. (2000), *Cultivating Pluralism: Psychological, Social and Cultural Perspectives on a Changing Ireland*, Dublin: Oak Tree Press.

MacLachlan, M. (ed.) (2001), *Cultivating Health: Cultural Perspectives on Promoting Health*, Chichester: Wiley.

MacLachlan, M. (2003a), "Cultural Dynamics: Transition and Identity in Modern Ireland", in M. Hederman-O'Brien (ed.), *Mosaic or Melting Pot?* Dublin: European Cultural Foundation & Royal Irish Academy.

MacLachlan, M. (2003b), "Health, Empowerment and Culture" in M. Murray (ed.), *Critical Health Psychology*, London: Sage.

MacLachlan, M. Smyth, C.L., Madden, T., and Breen, F. (submitted), *Temporal Acculturation and Mental Health in Modern Ireland*.

Marin, M.P.U. (1999), "Where Development will lead to Mass Suicide", *The Ecologist*, 29, 42-46.

Metge, J. (1995), *New Growth from Old*, Wellington: Victoria University Press.

Michel, K. and Valach, L. (2001)," Suicide as Goal-Directed Action" in K. van Heeringen (ed.), *Understanding Suicidal Behaviour*, Chichester: John Wiley and Sons.

Michel, K., Valach, L. and Waeber, V. (1994), "Understanding deliberate self-harm: the patients' views", *Crisis*, 15, 172-178.

Miller, D.N. and DuPaul, G.J. (1996), "School-based prevention of adolescent suicide: Issues, obstacles, and recommendations for practice", *Journal of Emotional and Behavioural Disorders*, 4, 221-230.

Miller, D.N., Eckert, T.L., DuPaul, G.J. and White, G.P. (1999), "Adolescent Suicide Prevention: Acceptability of School-Based Programs among Secondary School Principals", *Suicide and Life-Threatening Behaviour*, 29(1), 72-85.

Morselli, H. (1903), *Suicide: An Essay in Comparative Moral Statistics*, New York: Appleton.

National Council for Curriculum and Assessment (2002), *Review of Exploring Masculinities: Final Report*, Dublin: Government Publications.

Novins, D.K., Beals, J., Roberts, R.E. and Manson, S.M. (1999), "Factors associated with suicide ideation among American Indian adolescents: Does culture matter?" *Suicide and Life-Threatening Behaviour*, 29(4), 332-346.

O'Carroll, P.W., Berman, A.L., Maris, R., Moscicki, E., Tanney, B. and Silverman, M. (1998), "Beyond the tower of Babel: A nomenclature for suicide", in R.J. Kosky, H.S. Eshkevari, R.D. Goldney and R. Hassan (eds.), *Suicide Prevention: The Global Context*, New York: Plenum.

O'Connell, M. (2001), *Changed Utterly: Ireland and the New Irish Psyche*, Dublin: The Liffey Press.

O'Connor, R. (2001), *The Psychology of Suicidal Behaviour*, Paper presented at the Irish Association of Suicidology 6th Annual Conference, Derry, Ireland.

O'Connor, R. and Sheehy, N. (2000), *Understanding Suicidal Behaviour*, Leicester: British Psychological Society Books.

O'Donoghue, D.J. (1894), *The Humour of Ireland*, London: W. Scott.

Office of the Commissioner for Children (1996), "The Suicide Index: Deaths by Suicide and Self-Inflicted Injury per 100,000 or Population, ages 15-24, 1991-1993", *Children*, June 1996 (21).

Orbach, I. and Glaubman, H. (1978), "Suicidal, aggressive and normal children's perception of personal and impersonal death", *Journal of Clinical Psychology*, 34, 850-856.

Parrish, I. (1837), "Analecta: Case of suicide in a child", *Transylvania Journal of Medicine*, 10, 737-739.

Peltzer, K. (1995), *Psychology and Health in African Cultures: Examples of Ethnopsychotherapeutic Practice*, Frankfurt: IKO Verlag.

Peltzer, K. (2002), "Personality and Social Behaviour in Africa", *Journal of Personality and Social Behaviour*.

Pfeffer, C.R. (1986), *The Suicidal Child*, New York: Guilford.

Pfeffer, C.R., Conte, H.R., Plutchik, R. and Jerrett, I. (1979), "Suicidal behaviour in latency-age children: an empirical study", *Journal of the American Academy of Child and Adolescent Psychiatry*, 18, 679-692.

Pfeffer, C.R., Conte, H.R., Plutchik, R. and Jerrett, I. (1980), "Suicidal behaviour in latency-age children: an empirical study: an outpatient population", *Journal of the American Academy of Child and Adolescent Psychiatry*, 19, 703-710.

Pfeffer, C.R., Zuckerman, S., Plutchik, R. and Mizruchi, M.S. (1984), "Suicidal behaviour in normal school children: a comparison with child psychiatric inpatients", *Journal of the American Academy of Child and Adolescent Psychiatry*, 23, 416-423.

Phillips, D.P. (1974), "The influence of suggestion on suicide: Substantive and theoretical implications of the Werther effect", *American Sociological Review*, 39(3), 340-354.

Phillips, J. (1996), *A Man's Country* (2nd. ed.), Auckland: Penguin.

Piaget, J. (1965), *The Child's Conception of the World*, Ottawa, NT: Littlefield Adams.

Pounder, D.J. (1991), "Changing patterns of male suicide in Scotland", *Forensic Science International*, 51(1), 79-87.

Prilleltensky, I. and Nelson, G. (2002), *Doing Psychology Critically: Making a Difference in Diverse Settings*, Basingstoke: Palgrave.

Range, L.M., Leach, M.M., McIntyre, D., Posey-Deters, P.B., Marion, M.S., Kovac, S.H., Banos, J.H. and Vigil, J. (1999), "Multicultural Perspectives on Suicide", *Aggression and Violent Behaviour*, 4(4), 413-430.

Raviv, A., Bal-Tar, D., Ravic, A. and Ben-Horin, A. (1996), "Adolescent idolization of pop singers: Causes, expressions and reliance" *Journal of Youth and Adolescence*, 25(5), 63-650.

Reinherz, H.Z., Giaconia, R.M., Pakiz, B., Silverman, A., Frost, A. and Lefkowitz, E.S. (1993), "Psychological risks for major depression in late adolescence: a longitudinal community study", *Journal of the American Academy of Child and Adolescent Psychiatry*, 32, 1155-1163.

Reinherz, H.Z., Giaconia, R.M., Silverman, A., Friedman, A., Pakiz, B., Frost, A. and Choen, E. (1995), "Early Psychosocial Risks for Adolescent Suicidal Ideation and Attempts", *Journal of the American Academy of Child and Adolescent Psychiatry*, 34(5), 599-611.

Reynolds, W.M. and Mazza, J.J. (1994), "Suicide and suicidal behaviours in children and adolescents" in W.M. Reynolds and H.F. Johnston (eds.), *Handbook of Depression in Children and Adolescents*, New York: Plenum Press.

Rice, F. (1996), *The Adolescent: Development, relationships and Culture* (7th ed.), Boston: Allyn and Bacon.

Rich, C.L., Young, D. and Fowler, R.C. (1986), "San Diego Suicide Study: Young v. Old Subjects", *Archives of General Psychiatry*, 43, 577-582.

Ritchie, J. and Ritchie, J. (1979), *Growing up in Polynesia*, Sydney: Allen & Unwin.

Robertson, I. (1990), *Social Problems*, New York: Random House.

Rorty, A.O. (1976), *The Identities of Persons*, Berkeley: University of California Press.

Rosenblatt, A., Greenberg, J., Solomon, S., Pyszczynski, T. and Lyon, D. (1989), "Evidence for Terror Management Theory I: The Effects of Mortality Salience on Reactions to Those Who Violate or Uphold Cultural Values", *Journal of Personality and Social Psychology*, 57, 681-690.

Ryan, A.S. (1985), "Cultural factors in casework with Chinese Americans", *Social Work: The Journal of Contemporary Social Work*, 15, 333-340.

Schwimmer, E. (1968), *The Maori People in the Nineteen Sixties*, Sydney/Auckland: Blackwood and Janet Paul.

Seca, J.M. (1991), "Les purificateurs du rock", *Cahiers Internationaux de Sociologie*, 90(38), 121-130.

Shaffer, D., Garland, A., Gould, M., Fisher, P. and Trautman, P. (1988), "Preventing teenage suicide: A critical review", *Journal of the American Academy of Child and Adolescent Psychiatry*, 27, 675-687.

Shneidman, E.S. (1985), *Definitions of Suicide*, New York: Wiley.

Shneidman, E.S. (1990), "Preventing Suicide" in J. Donnelly (ed.), *Suicide: Right or Wrong?* New York: Prometheus Books.

Showalter, E. (1997), *Hystories: Hysterical Epidemics and Modern Culture*, London: Picador.

Silviny, H. (1957), "Suicide and the Law" in E.S. Shneidman and N.L. Fareberow (eds.), *Clues to Suicide*, New York: McGraw-Hill.

Smyth, C.L. and MacLachlan, M. (2002), *Berry Across Time — Temporal Acculturation and Mental Health in Modern Ireland*, Paper presented at the XVI Congress of the International Association for Cross-Cultural Psychology: *Unity in Diversity: Enhancing a Peaceful World*, Yogyakarta, Java: Indonesia.

Solomon, S., Greenberg, J. and Pyszczynski, T. (1991), "A Terror Management Theory of Social Behaviour: The psychological functions of self-esteem and cultural worldviews", *Advances in Experimental Social Psychology*, 24, 93-159.

Solomon, S., Greenberg, J. and Pyszczynski, T. (1998), "Tales from the Crypt: On the role of death in life", *Zygon*, 33, 9-43.

Speece, M. and Brent, S. (1992), "The acquisition of a mature understanding of three components of the concept of death", *Death Studies*, 16, 221-229.

Spellissy, S. (1996), *Suicide: The Irish Experience*, Cork: On-Stream Publications.

Stack, S. (1998), "Heavy Metal, Religiosity and Suicide Acceptability" *Suicide and Life-Threatening Behaviour*, 28(4), 388-394.

Stack, S., Gundkach, J. and Reeves, J.L. (1994), "The heavy metal subculture and suicide", *Suicide and Life-Threatening Behaviour*, 24, 5-23.

Stillion, J. and McDowell, E. (1996), *Suicide Across the Lifespan* (2nd ed.), Washington, DC: Taylor & Francis.

Stone, G. (1999), *Suicide and Attempted Suicide*, New York: Carroll and Graf Publishers.

Takahashi, Y. (1997), "Culture and Suicide: From a Japanese Psychiatrist's Perspective", *Suicide and Life-Threatening Behaviour*, 27(1), 137-145.

Taylor, S. (1982), *Durkheim and the Study of Suicide*, London: The Macmillan Press Ltd.

Tosh, J. (1999), *A Man's Place: Masculinity and the Middle Class Home in Victorian England*, London: Yale University Press.

Trotter, T. (1807), *A View of the Nervous Temperament . . .*, Newcastle: Walker, for Longman, Hurst, Rees and Orme.

Unger, R.K. and Crawford, M. (1996), *Women and Gender: A Feminist Psychology* (2nd ed.), New York: McGraw- Hill.

Weinstein, D. (1991), *Heavy Metal: A Cultural Sociology*, New York: Macmillan.

Williams, J.M. (1986), "Differences in reasons for taking overdoses in high and low hopelessness groups", *British Journal of Medical Psychology*, 59, 269-277.

Williams, J.M.G. and Pollock, L.R. (2000), "The Psychology of Suicidal Behaviour" in K. Hawton and K. van Heeringen (eds.), *International Handbook of Suicide and Attempted Suicide*, Chichester: John Wiley and Sons.

World Health Organisation (2001), *The World Health Report 2002: Mental Health: New Understanding, New Hope*, Geneva: WHO.

World Health Organisation (2002), *Suicide Rates*, Retrieved 26 September 2002 from WHO Website: http://www5.who.int/mental_health.

Index

acculturation, 31, 33, 35–6, 50–1, 78–81
assimilation, 50
integration, 50
marginalisation, 50
separation, 50
suicidal behaviour and, 78–81
temporal, 50–1, 80–1
theory, 50
uncertainty/cultural ambivalence, 47, 50–1
see also under culture; Irish culture; prevention; suicide
adolescence; *see* youth suicide
Aguilera, Christina, 112
alcohol, 33–4, 35, 40, 68, 69, 74, 83, 84, 94–6, 113
Amit-Talai, V., 72
Anatomy Act (1832), 16
anomie, 51–5
Aotearoa/New Zealand, 36–40
Aquinas, Thomas, 8
Aries, P., 63
Arnett, J., 60, 73
Ashe, Thomas, 21
Augustine, St, 7

Baker, W.E., 46
Bancroft, J., 118
Barber, J.G., 38
Beautrais, A.L., 25, 69, 70
Beck, Aaron, 91, 92
Beck Hopelessness Scale, 91
Becker, Ernest, 41
Berry, John, 35, 50, 79
Bible, 7–8
Boergers, J., 70, 71
Bowers, F., 20
Brent, S., 64
Browne, Sir Thomas, 6
Bryson, B., 74

Canetto, S.S., 84, 85, 86
Caplan, G., 120
Carr, S.C., 123
case study, 1–3
Casualty, 77–8
Catholic Church, 7–9, 19, 22, 48, 53–4; *see also under* Irish culture; suicide
Chandler, M.J., 80–1
child abuse, 110, 114
childhood suicide, 61–6, 114–15
concepts of death, 63–5
Piagetian theory, 63–4
preformation theory, 62–3
risk factors, 65–6
see also youth suicide
Church councils, 8

Church, role of the; *see under* suicide
Clare, Anthony, 83, 89, 92, 97, 98
Cobain, Kurt, 75–6, 78
Cole, D., 91
Colombia, 40
communication, 117–18
Coroner's Act (1962), 16
Coupe, N.M., 107
criminalisation, 5, 16–17
Criminal Law (Suicide) Act (1993), 16
Cúchulainn, 18
cultural
  ambivalence, 50–1
  continuity, 78–81
  diversity, 79
  evolution, 45–6
  icons, 59, 110, 111–12, 113
  identity, 3–4, 59, 111–14, 123–4
culture, 3–6, 29–55
  African American culture, 31, 32–3
  as facilitating factor, 30
  as protective factor, 30
  definition of culture, 29
  functions of, 40–5
    culture as mortality buffer, 26, 44–5
    self-esteem as anxiety buffer, 43
  homicide and suicide, 32
  Irish culture; *see* culture change; Irish culture
  Japanese culture, 39
  Maori culture, 36–40
  Native American culture, 31, 33–6
  U'wa people, 40–1
  see also culture change; Irish culture; suicide
culture change, 3, 45–55, 124
  ambivalence, 113–14
  anomie and suicide, 51–5
  impact of, 26, 45–7
  Ireland, 3, 5, 47, 48–51, 54–5, 81
  "transitional people", 46
  uncertainty, 47
Curran, D.K., 9, 30, 57, 58, 73

Daly, John, 21
death, concepts of, 39–40, 63–5; *see also* mortality, concerns about
Deirdre of the Sorrows, 17
Demos, J., 90
Department of Education and Science, 99–106, 124
Department of Health and Children, 95
de Valera, Éamon, 22
Dickens, Charles, 77
Diekstra, R.F.W., 10
Dominian, J., 62
Dracula, 20
drug abuse, 69, 94, 113
DuPaul, G.J., 119
Durkheim, Emile, 38, 51–4, 77

Early, K.E., 32
EchoHawk, 33, 34, 35–6
Eckersley, R., 107, 123
education; *see under* gender; prevention
Education Act (1998), 101
Elias, M.J., 120
Ellis, J.B., 86
Empty Raincoat, The, 3

fatherhood, changing nature of, 89–91
felo de se, 20

feminism, 87
Freud, Anna, 60
Freud, Sigmund, 41

Gaines, D., 75
gender and suicide, 6, 18, 22, 34, 36–8, 48, 68–71, 83–106, 112
  Balance: Who Cares? programme, 100, 101, 102, 105, 106
  biology, hormones and suicide, 96–8
  definition of gender, 84
  Exploring Masculinities programme, 99–106, 123, 124
  female patterns, 69, 92–4
  male risk, 83, 92–8
  masculinity, 37–8, 86, 87–92, 96–7, 99–106, 112
    historical construction, 87–91
  youth suicide, 68–71
Giddens, Anthony, 59, 111
Glaubman, H., 65
Gleeson, Jim, 100, 101
Goldney, R.D., 78
Grian (Gile Gréine), 18

Haim, A., 60
Hall, G. Stanley, 60
Handy, Charles, 3
Harry, J., 86
Hawton, K., 70, 77
Hovey, J., 79
Hume, David, 7
"hystories", 85

industrial revolution, 90
Inglehart, R., 46
Irish Association of Suicidology, 76
Irish Constitution, 90, 105
Irish culture, 3, 47, 48–51, 54–5, 59, 110, 111, 125
  Catholic Church, 20–1, 54
  "Celtic Tiger" acculturation, 47, 48–51, 54–5
  contemporary suicide, 22–7
  economic change and suicide, 48–9
  "fasting upon the enemy", 21
  folklore and mythology of suicide, 15–19, 20–1
  language, 15
  republican hunger strikes, 21–2
  traditional burial of suicides, 19–20
Irish Times, The, 94, 105
Isometsa, E.T., 117

Janssen, J., 73
Jenkins, R., 115
Judas Iscariot, 7, 8

Kalafat, J., 120, 121
Kane, B., 63
Kastenbaum, 64
Kazarian, S.S., 78–9
Kelleher, Michael, 8, 16, 20, 21, 22, 25–6, 51
Kelly, F., 21
Kenny, C., 59, 61, 62, 63, 64
Kim, U., 79
King, C.A., 79
King, S.R., 74
Klein, Naomi, 59
Kopp, Sheldon, 42
Kosky, R.J., 11, 12
Kraemer, S., 96
Kumar, G., 92

Lalonde, C., 80–1

Langford, R.A., 37, 40
language, 10–13, 15, 38, 76–7
Leonard, E.C., 77
Lester, David, 29, 74
Lewis, R.J., 86
Linehan, M.M., 86
Lourie, R.S., 62

MacLachlan, Malcolm, 1, 30, 31, 42, 45, 45, 47, 48, 50, 88, 111, 114, 124
Mazza, J.J., 119
McDowell, E., 9, 65, 66, 114
MacSwiney, Terence, 22
men and masculinity; *see* gender
methods of suicide, 23–5
  availability hypothesis, 23
  drowning, 23, 24
  firearms, 23, 24, 25, 34
  hanging, 23, 24, 25, 34
  self-poisoning, 23, 24, 25
  see also prevention
Michel, K., 115–16, 118
Miller, D.N., 118, 119
Morselli, H., 52
mortality, concerns about, 41–5; *see also* death, concepts of; terror management theory

National Council for Curriculum and Assessment (NCCA), 101
National Suicide Review Group, 25
National Task Force on Suicide, 22
Nelson, G., 108
New Zealand; *see* Aotearoa/ New Zealand
Nirvana, 75
No Logo, 59
Novins, D.K., 33
*N'SYNC, 112

O'Carroll, P.W., 11, 13
O'Connell, M., 47, 48, 59
O'Connor, R., 6, 30, 67
Orbach, I., 65
Organisation for Economic Cooperation and Development (OECD), 36
Osbourne, Ozzy, 74

Parrish, I., 77
Peltzer, K., 46
Persad, E., 78–9
Pfeffer, C.R., 65
Phillips, D.P., 37
Piaget, J., 63–4
Pickwick Papers, The, 77
Pounder, D.J., 25
prevention, 5, 22, 23, 107–8, 115–23
  action theory approach, 115–17
  availability hypothesis, 23, 25
  barriers to prevention, 117–19
  cultural continuity, 26, 78–81
  methods of suicide; *see* methods of suicide
  role of the media, 75–8, 123
  school-based prevention, 5, 22, 23, 99–106, 118–23, 124
    recommendations, 121–2
    types, 119–20
Prilleltensky, I., 108
"psychache", 11, 18, 106

"race" and ethnicity, 31
Range, L.M., 31, 32, 33, 34, 86
Rank, Otto, 41
Raviv, A., 74
Reinherz, H.Z., 68–9
"relative misery hypothesis", 38
Religio Medici, 6
Reynolds, W.M., 119

Rice, F., 72
Robertson, I., 58
Rousseau, Jean-Jacques, 7

Sands, Bobby, 21–2
Seca, J.M., 73
self-esteem, 43, 69, 73, 89
Shaffer, D., 119
Sheehy, N., 6, 67
Shepeard, G., 86
Shneidman, Edwin, 6, 7, 8, 10, 13, 17, 62, 71, 106
Showalter, E., 85
Singh, B., 115
Smyth, Caroline, 114
socialisation, 85, 96–7
Solomon, S., et al., 41–2, 43–5
Spears, Britney, 112
Speece, M., 64
Spellissy, Sean, 6, 9, 15–21
Stack, S., 74
Steer, R.A., 92
Stillion, J., 9, 65, 66, 114
Stoker, Bram, 20
suicide
  "altruistic", 53
  ancient Greek, 6
  ancient Roman, 6
  biomedical approach, 4–5, 26, 67, 96–8, 115, 116–17, 118, 119
  culture-based definition, 62
  culture-based understanding, 3, 4–5, 26, 29–31, 52–3, 67, 78, 81, 84, 107–17, 123–5; *see also* acculturation; culture; Irish culture; suicide, schematic of factors leading to
  "causes" and "reasons", 118
  definitions of, 5, 10–13, 62
  gender and; *see* gender and suicide
  history of, 5, 6–10, 15–22
  hopelessness and depression, 68, 75, 86, 91–2, 94, 96, 102
  in Ireland, 15–27, 83, 92–4; *see also* Irish culture
  Irish statistics, 22–6, 83, 92–4
    reliability of, 25–6
  medical attitudes, 16–17, 97–8, 117
  phenomenological approach, 61, 71
  prevention; *see* prevention
  proximate and ultimate causes, 108–10
  religion and, 6–9, 39, 46, 53–4, 74
  traditional psychology and psychiatry, 30, 52–3, 115–18
  use of term
    in Ireland, 15–16, 17
    medieval, 6
    philosophy, 7
    Roman Catholic church, 7–9, 19, 22
    youth; *see* youth suicide
Suicide, Le (Durkheim), 51, 77
suicide-related behaviours, 11–13, 61, 65, 67–72, 77, 84, 85–7, 91–2, 116
  as goal-directed action, 116
  attempted suicide, 12, 70, 85–6
    as a "cry for help", 71–2, 85–6
  gender and, 68–71, 84, 85–7, 91–2
  ideation, 68, 69, 74
  precipitating experiences, 70, 96
  proposed nomenclature, 11–13
  self-harm, 5

suicide, schematic of factors leading to, 107–15
 culture and community, 110, 112–14
 family, 110, 114–15
 globalisation, 110, 111–12
 proximate factors, 108–9, 110
 self, 110, 115
suicide trajectory model, 65–6, 114

Taylor, Steve, 51, 52
temporal acculturation, 50–1, 80–1
 theory, 50–1
terror management theory, 41–2
thanatology, 64
Trotter, T., 77

uncertainty, 47, 50–1, 59
UNICEF, 36
United States, 31, 32–36, 111–12, 120

Valach, L., 115–16, 118

Weinstein, D., 74
Werther effect, 75
Whipple, M., 74
Williams, J.M., 71
World Health Organisation, 10, 13
World Values Survey, 46–7

youth culture, 72–8, 112
 death and, 73
 definition, 72
 heavy metal and suicide, 73–5
 media coverage and copycat suicides, 75–8
 protective role, 73
youth suicide, 6, 36–7, 57–81, 117–23
 adolescence, 57–61, 112
  as newly created life-stage, 57–9
  pathologising, 60–1
  "storm and stress", 60
 early experiences and, 67–72
 identifying risk, 117–23
 male suicide; *see* gender
 postmodern changes, 59
 reasons for suicide, 67–72
  as a cry for help, 71–2
  explicit wish to die, 71–2
 risk factors, 67–72, 117–23
 role of the family, 114–15